American Journals

American Journals
Albert Camus

Translation by Hugh Levick

PARAGON HOUSE PUBLISHERS
New York

First English translation, 1987.

Published by
PARAGON HOUSE PUBLISHERS
90 Fifth Avenue
New York, New York 10011
Copyright 1987 by Paragon House Publishers
Copyright 1978 by Éditions Gallimard

Cover and text design by Edward A. Butler

Library of Congress Cataloging-in-Publication Data

Camus, Albert, 1913–1960.
   American journals.

   Translation of: Journaux de voyage.
     1. Camus, Albert, 1913–1960—Journeys—America.
2. Authors, French—20th century—Biography.
3. America—Description and travel.   I. Title.
PQ2605.A3734Z46613   1987   848′.91403 [B]   87–2376
ISBN 0-913729-68-X

Contents

Preface to the English Language Edition

American Journals is a translation of *Journaux de voyage*, which was published by Gallimard in 1978. The complete text has been translated, with the exception of several explanatory notes unnecessary for English-language readers. Some notes have also been added, to identify names and terms perhaps more familiar to French readers than to those reading in English.

The volume incorporates two of Camus's notebooks: one kept during his 1946 visit to the

United States, and the second, during his 1949 trip to South America. The United States journal, which is the shorter of the two, is loosely structured: Camus seems to be writing when the mood strikes him. Entries are generally labelled by days of the week or descriptive headings. In contrast, every entry in the South American journal begins with a date, and there is an entry for every date, except July 29, and August 28-30 (during the latter period, Camus was ill and anxious to return to Paris, his departure having been postponed several times).

These journals reflect the stress of travel and a hectic schedule of public appearances, and thus they afford us glimpses of Camus at his most sardonic *and* his most vulnerable. Witness his first reaction to New York: ". . . Everyone looks like they've stepped out of a B-film"; and his thoughts during the sea voyage to South America: "Twice, the idea of suicide . . . I think I understand now *how* one kills oneself." Camus's attitude toward the sea best expresses his ambivalence: "That's the way the sea is, and that's why I love it! A call to life and an invitation to death!" The journals are filled with humorous observations, somber musings on philosophy and the meaning of life, and notes which would later become parts of larger works, including "The Growing Stone," "The Sea Close By," *Neither Victims nor Executioners* and *The Plague*.

The introduction which follows was written by Roger Quilliot, a long-time editor of Camus, who compiled the *Pléiade* edition of Camus's works.

Introduction to the French Edition

Several years ago, when we published the second volume of Albert Camus's *Notebooks*, two difficulties presented themselves: one a problem of principle, the other technical in nature.

The notebook devoted to South America was not filed with the others; the manuscript was also separate.[1] It was entitled *Voyage to South America*. It was clear that the author had questioned himself about its fate. Furthermore, when in 1954 he sent me the typed manuscript of these collected

Notebooks, the trip to South America appeared in a special folder. Had Camus envisaged fleshing it out, making of it a larger work? We have no proof. But everything indicates that the trip and its narration occupied a special place in his mind.

This being the case, in what form could we publish it, since the notebook itself was too short to come out as an individual volume? Very logically, we imagined associating it with a trip to North America which was included in the chronological sequence of the other notebooks.[2] An inclusion which is easy to understand if one considers that aside from some traveller's notes concerning the crossing of the Atlantic and the discovery of New York, Camus speaks rather little about the meetings and adventures that constituted this voyage, and even less about the lectures he gave in New York and at Harvard and how people reacted to them. On the other hand, the preoccupations that are strewn throughout the 1945 and 1946 notebooks are present in these pages, in particular *The Plague.*

Despite these differences in texture we decided to issue the two notebooks together. The text was established by Madame Camus and myself by examining different typescripts and manuscripts, one of which—the notebook of the Voyage to the U.S.A.—belonged, like all the note-books of its type, to Madame Camus, the other to Madame Maria Casarès, who generously entrusted it to us for examination.

To avoid all useless speculation, let me say once again that these texts are published, like those which preceded them, without any cuts. Initials, when they exist, were chosen by the author. One exception, however: twice we have replaced the name of the same person with an X.

•

The two notebooks have one point of interest in common: they show us how Camus passed from rough notes to a finished work. Several passages from the Voyage to the U.S.A. can be found in "The Rains of New York"; important fragments from the Voyage to South America have been integrated either into "The Sea Close By" (*L'Éte*), or even more voluminously into "The Growing Stone." Two dance scenes, actually witnessed, are condensed into one of the only exotic texts which Camus ever wrote; the trip to Iguape and the episode of the growing stone, recorded as simple folklore, take on, in the short story, symbolic value. There are few examples which so clearly exhibit the transformations of the raw fact into the created myth—and it is a myth willed optimistic by the author, for whom the actual voyage was exhausting and depressing.

The different circumstances of the two voyages influenced Camus's reactions: the trip to the U.S.A., begun March 10, 1946, is the voyage of a well-known journalist who has not yet attained full recognition as an author. From which fact springs the wary welcome of the American immigration police who see in Camus the moving spirit behind a newspaper which proudly flaunts the motto, *From Resistance to Revolution*. The amazing thing is that Camus tells us nothing about his visits to the American universities, which should have been astonishing for a French traveller, nor about the most prestigious of them, Harvard, which nonetheless recorded his passage in its monthly bulletin. His notes suggest a kind of bewilderment, both admiring and reproachful, face to face with this New World, limitless both in its skyscrapers and its expanses; and a vague anxiety about the unconscious expansionism implied by such colossal power. In the near future, between the two hostile camps forming in the East and the West—of which the U.S.A. is one of the pillars—Camus will obstinately refuse to choose. Nonetheless, at this time he confides to his former teacher, M. Germain: "My trip to America taught me a lot of things, the details of which would take more space than I have here. It's a great country, strong and disciplined in liberty, but unaware of many things, foremost of which is Europe."

The Voyage to South America is of a different nature: Camus is in a precarious state of health at the outset, but it is only progressively that he begins to suspect a new attack of tuberculosis. In this sense his itinerary is also that of the re-emerging illness, which is one of the subjects of "The Sea Close By." He cannot be far from those who are dear to him without great pain, to which his nervousness about mail delays testifies. Finally, it is his first official voyage as a celebrity: they will not get him to do it again (although later on he, in reality, gives lectures in Italy and Greece). If he does manage to amuse himself from time to time, more often than not he is annoyed by the many constraints inherent in this kind of project: a variety of meetings, often disappointing, the uneven quality of his hosts and how he is received— everything is set up to irritate a man who detests fashionable gatherings, but who knows that having undertaken this trip, he must also accept these annoyances. Thus we see him submitting himself, with vexation, to an excessively busy schedule of events of varying degrees of interest.

On the whole these pages bear the mark of a state of crisis which is confirmed from the very beginning as he reads Vigny on the boat. It is a physical crisis which will take Camus many months to overcome; an existential crisis which translates into his obsession with suicide and his acute feeling of exile—another aspect of this voyage which places it at the source of "The Growing Stone."

He also appears to be particularly sensitive to the intense contrasts within these American lands, as seen from a European vantage point: wealth and extreme poverty; refined and primitive cultures, sometimes within the same community. Not to mention the enormous problem that the over-population of these lands—particularly in the large cities—poses for any lucid observer! Not without discomfort does Camus discover what was beginning to be called the Third World. And without a doubt he suffers from seeing it in a whirl of airplane flights and fashionable gatherings.

•

Two trips separated from one another by a span of three years. During the twelve years which follow, Camus rarely consents to lectures in foreign countries: he will refuse a huge sum from Japan. Only from a sense of obligation will he resign himself to the Nobel Prize celebrations in Stockholm, and even then only at the insistence of Roger Martin du Gard and his publishers.

Paradoxically, even though the young man without great resources had travelled freely throughout Europe, the writer at the height of his

fame, after 1948, gave up the voyages which generally enriched the lives of his contemporaries.

R. Quilliot

1. It is announced in the manuscript of notebook VI by the indica-
tion, "see S. Am. journal June to August 1949."

2. In manuscript these pages are found in notebook V, a student
notebook like the preceding ones, and the text is connected to the
page which was begun before his departure. In the two typescripts,
the numbering of the pages does not indicate any discontinuity. In-
contestably, the notes were made spontaneously, and were not re-
written.

The United States

March - May, 1946.

• AMERICA. DEPARTURE.

The light anxiety of departure has passed. In the train, I meet R., a psychiatrist who is going over there to make contacts. I know that he'll be in my cabin on the boat, and that's all right because I find him both discreet and friendly. In my train compartment, three kids rather wild at the start, but who eventually calm down, their little maid, their mother, a tall, elegant woman with bright eyes, and a tiny little blond woman who sits opposite me crying. An uneventful trip except for one incident. I do several favors for the young blond woman. Before Rouen, a sort of tall woman with thick features, dressed in a long fur coat, asks me if all the people in this part of the train are going to America. If I'm going. "Yes." She excuses herself and then asks me if she can ask me what I'm going to do there.

"Some lectures."

"Literary or scientific?"

"Literary."

A truly theatrical exclamation, complete with raising her hand quickly to cover her mouth—escapes her. "Ah!" she says, "isn't that marvelous!"

And two seconds later, her eyes lowered: "I am also in literature."

"Oh, really!"

"Yes. I am going to publish a book of poems."

"That's very good," I say.

"Yes, and I've gotten Rosemonde Gérard to contribute a preface. She's written a very beautiful sonnet for me."

"That's wonderful!"

"Of course, it's only my first book. But to make a literary debut with a preface by Rosemonde Gérard. . . ."

"Who's the publisher?"

She gives me a name that I don't know. She explains that it's traditional verse "because my leaning is towards the classical forms. I don't know what you think about modern literature ... but I don't like what I can't understand," etc., etc. She gets off the train at Rouen and offers to mail a telegram for me that I want to send to Paris because I've left behind R's New York address. She never sent it because I haven't received an answer.

In the dining car I see R. and we eat lunch sitting opposite the tiny blond who can't manage to crack her walnuts. In Le Havre the tiny little woman, who seems completely lost, asks me to help her. Waiting for the bus we talk a little. She's going to Philadelphia. The bus is an old police van, dirty and dusty. Le Havre, with its immense ruins. The air is hot and humid. When we arrive at the Oregon, I see that it's a freighter, a large freighter, but a freighter nonetheless. Customs, foreign exchange, police station with the small box of cards that a cop checks while you tell him your name—and that I know well because of some close calls that I had with boxes like this one during the occupation. And then boarding the ship.

The cabin for four with showers and a toilet has become a cabin for five where it's impossible to sneeze without knocking something over. We are asked to go to the dining room to see the maitre d'hotel. In reality we've been convened to watch a comic performance. The maitre d'hotel looks like the Frenchmen that one sees in American films, and on top of it, he's afflicted with a tic that has him passing out irritating winks right and left. In order to compose harmonious dining tables he has, like a good hostess, a layout of the dining room and a list of the professions of those passengers who've come specially recommended. Naturally, he wants to put me with a journalist.[1] But I refuse energetically and finally manage to get a table with R. and the little blond whose name is—wonderfully—Jeanne Lorette. She's a little Parisian who's in the perfume business, who was crying this morning because she had left her twin sister who's everything to her, but she's going to Philadelphia to meet an American whom she's supposed to marry. R. is delighted by the naturalness, discretion, and kindness of Lorette. Me too. We're a little less delighted by the cabin. The foldout bed, in the middle of the room, is occupied by an old man of 70. The bunk above mine belongs to a middle-aged guy whom I take to be a businessman. Above R. is a vice consul who's on his way to Shanghai and who has an open, fun-loving appearance. We get settled and then I decide to do some work.

I dine with R., Lorette, the tall lady from the train compartment (she's not really so tall—but thin and elegant), and a Mexican couple "who are in business." The two women seem to look at our Lorette a little distrustfully. But since she just continues being natural, she's the one who appears to have the most class. She tells us that her mother-in-law who doesn't even know her sends her the nicest letters, and that it seems that American mothers-in-law are absolutely top quality. Her fiancé is religious, and he neither drinks nor smokes. He asked her to go to confession before leaving France. The morning she was leaving (during the preceding days, she had been getting the necessary papers, etc.) she got up at 6 A.M. to go to church, but it was closed and the train was leaving early. So she'll confess over there and, she says in her light Parisian accent (most of the time she articulates very badly and you have to strain to catch what she's saying), "I prefer that because the one over there won't understand very well what I'm saying, and he'll give me absolution." We explain to her that in cases like this they always give absolution. "Even for mortal ones." But of course, R. says, convinced. And we point out to her the fact that there's undoubtedly a chaplain on the boat.

After dinner R. and I agree on the fact that the charming Lorette tries to calm her own apprehension by presenting to others and consequently to herself a comforting image of her situation—which is perhaps comforting, but this is not the question. In any case we also agree on wishing for this curious little creature all the happiness that she deserves. Going to sleep is a more difficult project. The cabin is packed. There are two snorers, the old man and the businessman. On top of that R. and I had opened the porthole, but the old man closes it in the middle of the night. I have the impression that I'm breathing the breath of the others and I want to go sleep on the deck. Only the idea of the cold holds me back. Wake up at 7:30 A.M. because after 8:30 we can no longer have breakfast. Work in the morning. At 12:15 lunch. The Mexican tells me that he represents French perfumes in Mexico and goes on and on about French quality. The beautiful bright eyes opposite me lose a little of their haughtiness, and one perceives that there was a lot of timidity in their brilliance. Lorette assures us that she will never permit her family to speak badly of France. She portrays the people of Antwerp as having outstanding judgement. (If they buy jewels for their wives, they're always uncut diamonds, never set rings. That way, they have capital. And fur coats. Safe investments in short.)

In the afternoon we speak with the vice-consul. I'm not surprised to learn that he is from Oran. And naturally we pat each other enthusiastically on the shoulder. He's been to the most unbelievable countries, among them Bolivia, which he describes very well. La Paz is at an altitude of 13,000 feet. Automobiles there lose 40% of their power, tennis balls hardly make it over the net, and horses can only jump low obstacles. He managed there by eating garlic. His wife, a cultivated Polish woman, tells R. stories about magic. 3 P.M. The ship leaves. The sea is smooth. The wife of one of the sailors, in full mourning, runs clumsily down the pier waving goodbye to the ship. My last image of France is of destroyed buildings at the very edge of a wounded earth.

• T O W O R K.

At dinner the Mexican tells stories about passing through customs. Only one is interesting: the one about an American in Mexico who, after an accident, wanted to bring his defunct leg back with him in a crystal box. Three days of discussions to know whether or not this object fell into a category which had been established to restrict the importation of materials that could lead to epidemics. But the American having declared that he would remain in Mexico rather than be separated from his leg, the United States took action so as not to lose an honorable citizen. Lorette coughs a lot and is afraid of getting seasick. R. wants to cure her through autosuggestion. Which he does very skillfully. After dinner I have a drink with Madame D., the tall, bright-eyed woman. Husband at the Washington Embassy.

• 10 A.M. TUESDAY.

The night was short but good. This morning it's raining and the sea is swelling. The bar is practically empty. I work in peace. The Atlantic is the color of a pigeon's wing. Before lunch I lie down, my stomach a little upset, and after sleeping for half an hour, I wake up fresh as a daisy. At lunch some abstentions. Our Lorette stays in her bunk all day. The Mexicans leave the table before the end of the meal. Mme. D., R. and I enjoy a friendly chat. But R. is a little uncomfortable and goes to lie down. And even though I feel fine, I do the same. I feel too sluggish to work. But I do read *War and Peace.* How I would have been in love with Natasha!

The day drags on, heavy and monotonous. After dinner Mr. X of the furs talks to me about Oriental wisdom. It's the kind of conversation that I've never been able to stand for more than five minutes. I leave to join Natasha Rostov in bed.

• WEDNESDAY.

Awake with a fever and a vague discomfort in my throat. Despite a rough sea the sun is beautiful. I spend the morning stretched out beneath it. In the afternoon English with R. on the bridge and cocktails with Mme. D. at the Captain's. After dinner R. tells me about his memories as a doctor. Dachau. Diarrhea flowing from the bodies of the dying piled one on top of the other.

• THURSDAY.

Lousy day with shivers from a flu. In the evening a little champagne with R. and Mme. D. revives me. But my head is empty. Nevertheless, English in the afternoon.

• FRIDAY.

The flu subsides. But life continues to be monotonous. I work a little in the morning. The sea still rough. In the afternoon together with the consul (Dahoui) we receive Mme. D. and L. in our cabin. An enjoyable conversation. The consul tells (with Algerian eloquence) the story of a little vice-consul from Andripole who was unable to pay his first visit to the consul because of four orangutans which were tied up in the consul's waiting room.

He finally decides to make the call, but continues to spend fearful days in the consulate. Finally, after the consul tells him that one of the animals had died from eating a box of matches, the vice-consul brings a box each day and gives it affectionately to one of the animals until its death is achieved. When all four of them are buried, he breathes easily again.

Also a classic story of consuls who've spent 30 years in Djeddah[2] and elsewhere, who drink and die in solitude (for me).

In the evening after dinner, since we are going to sail near the Azores, I go onto the deck and, in a corner sheltered from the strong wind which has been blowing since our departure, I revel in a pure night, with rare but enormous stars which pass quickly in a straight line above the ship. A slender moon gives the sky a light without brilliance which lights up the turbulent water with its reflection. Once again I look, as I have for years, at the designs that the foam and the wake make on the surface of the water, this lace which is incessantly made and unmade, this liquid marble . . . and once more I look for the exact comparison that will hold for me this marvelous flowering of sea, water, and light that has escaped me for so long now. Still in vain. For me, it's a recurring symbol.

• FRIDAY. SATURDAY. SUNDAY.

Same program. The sea still too rough, we head towards the South and pass the Azores. This society in miniature is both fascinating and dull. Everyone prides himself on being elegant and knowing how to live. The performing dog aspect. But some of them are opening up. The furrier X is on the boat. Thus we learn that he has a magnificent porcelain service, superb silver, etc., but that he uses copies that he's had made and keeps the originals locked up. Which made me think that he also has a copy of a wife with whom he's never been able to enjoy anything more than a copy of love.

Three or four passengers are obviously going to the U.S.A. to export capital. I even have the crafty strategy explained to me. "Notice," says one of them, "that I'm not doing anything against my country. Its intentions are good, but France doesn't know anything about business." These people, on the contrary, know about business. I share with R., who continues to be a charming companion, the opinion that the only contemporary problem is money. Ugly-looking customers . . . greed and impotence. Fortunately, there is the company of women. It's the basic truth. Mme. D. more and more charming. L. also.

• M O N D A Y.

Beautiful day. The wind has subsided. For the first
time, the sea is calm. The passengers come up
onto the deck like mushrooms after a rainfall. We
breathe easily. Evening a magnificent sunset. After dinner, moonlight on the sea. Mme. D. and I
agree that most people don't lead the lives that
they would like to lead and that it's a question of
cowardice.

• S U N D A Y.

They announce that we will arrive in the evening.
The week has gone by in a whirl. The evening of
Tuesday the 21st, our table decided to celebrate
the arrival of spring. Drinking until 4 A.M. The
next day as well. Forty-eight euphoric hours during which all relationships rushed forward to new
levels. Mme. D. is in revolt against her milieu. L.
confesses to me that she's going to make a marriage of reason. On Saturday we've left the Gulf
Stream and it gets terribly chilly. The time passes
very quickly, however, and actually I'm not in such
a hurry to arrive. I've finished my lecture. And
the rest of the time I look at the sea, and I talk,
mostly with R.—truly intelligent—and of course
Mme. D. and L.

Today at noon, we see land. Since this morning seagulls have been flying over the boat, seemingly suspended, immobile, above the decks. The first thing we see is Coney Island, which looks like the Porte d'Orleans. "It's St. Denis or Gennevilliers," L. says. It's absolutely true. In the cold, with the grey wind and the flat sky, it's all rather depressing. We'll drop anchor in the bay of the Hudson and we won't disembark until tomorrow morning. In the distance, the skyscrapers of Manhattan against a backdrop of mist. Deep down, I feel calm and indifferent, as I generally do in front of spectacles that don't move me.

• M O N D A Y.

Go to bed very late. Get up very early. We enter New York harbor. A terrific sight despite or because of the mist. The order, the strength, the economic power are there. The heart trembles in front of so much admirable inhumanity.

I don't disembark until 11 A.M., after long formalities during which I am the only one of all the passengers to be treated as suspect. The immigration officer ends by excusing himself for having detained me for so long.[3] "I was obliged to, but I can't tell you why." A mystery, but after five years of occupation!

Met by C., E., and an envoy from the consulate. C. unchanged. E. also. But in all this bustle, the goodbyes with L, Mme. D., and R. are rapid and perfunctory.

Tired. My flu comes back. And it's on shaky legs that I get the first impact of New York. At first glance, a hideous, inhuman city. But I know that one changes one's mind. A few details strike me: that the garbage men wear gloves, that the traffic moves in an orderly fashion without policemen at the intersections, etc., that no one ever has change in this country, and that everyone looks like they've stepped out of a B-film. In the evening, crossing Broadway in a taxi, tired and feverish, I am literally stupefied by the circus of lights. I am just coming out of five years of night, and this orgy of violent lights gives me for the first time the impression of a new continent. An enormous, 50-foot-high Camel billboard: a G.I. with his mouth wide open blows enormous puffs of *real* smoke. Everything is yellow and red. I go to bed sick in both body and soul, but knowing perfectly well that I will have changed my mind in two days.

• TUESDAY.

Wake up with fever. Incapable of going out before noon. A little better when E. arrives. I have lunch with him and D., a Hungarian journalist, in a French restaurant. I realize that I haven't noticed the skyscrapers; they've seemed so natural to me. It's a question of general proportions. And then also you can't live all the time looking up. Therefore you only have in your field of vision a reasonable proportion of stories. Magnificent food stores. Enough to make all of Europe drool. I admire the women in the street, the color of their dresses, and the colors—reds, yellows, greens—of all the taxis which look like insects in their Sunday best. As for the stores selling ties, you have to see it to believe it. So much bad taste hardly seems imaginable. D. affirms that Americans don't like ideas. That's what they say. I'm not so sure.

At 3 o'clock I go to see Regine Junier. Admirable old maid who sends me all her wealth because her father died of consumption at 27 and so . . . She lives in two rooms in the middle of an army of hats which she makes, and which are exceptionally ugly. But nothing tarnishes the generous and attentive heart that shows in each word that she speaks. I leave her, devoured by fever and unable to do anything but go to bed. So much for the other meetings.—Odor of New York—a perfume of iron and cement—the iron dominates.

In the evening dinner with L.M. at "Rubens." He tells me the story of his secretary, very "American Tragedy." Married to a man with whom she has two children, she and her mother discover that the husband is a homosexual. Separation. The mother, a puritanical Protestant, works on the daughter for months, breeding in her the idea that her children are degenerates. The idiot finally suffocates one and strangles the other. Declared incompetent, she is freed. L.M. gives me his personal theory about Americans. It's the fifteenth that I've heard.

At the corner of East 1st Street, little bar where a loud juke box smothers all the conversations. To have five minutes of silence, you have to put in five cents.

• WEDNESDAY.

A little better this morning. Visit from Liebling, of the *New Yorker*. Charming man. Chiaromonte[4] then Rube. The latter two and I have lunch in a French restaurant. In my opinion, Ch. talks about America like nobody else. I point out to him the "funeral homes." He tells me how they function. One way to know a country is to know how people die there. Here, everything is anticipated. "You die and we do the rest," say the advertisements.

The cemeteries are private property: "Hurry up and reserve your place." Everything happens in the store, transportation, ceremonies, etc. A dead man is a finished man.—At Gilson's, radio. Then at my hotel with Vercors, Thimerais, and O'Brien.[5] Tomorrow's lecture. At 6, a drink with Gral at the St. Regis. Returning, I walk down Broadway, lost in the crowd and the enormous, illuminated billboards. Yes, there is an American tragic. It's what has been oppressing me since I arrived here, but I still don't know what it's made from.

Bowery Street, side by side for a quarter of a mile shops selling wedding gowns. I eat alone in the restaurant where I had lunch. And I go back to write.

Negro question. We sent a diplomat from Martinique to the consulate here. He was lodged in Harlem. With regard to his French colleagues, he perceived for the first time that he was not of the same race.

Contradictory observation: in the bus a middle-class American sitting opposite me gets up to give his seat to an old Negro lady.

Impression of overflowing wealth. Inflation is here, an American says to me.

• THURSDAY.

The day spent dictating my lecture. In the evening a little stage fright, but I throw myself into it right away and the public is "hooked." But while I'm speaking someone lifts the box office receipts which were supposed to be given to French children. At the end O'Brien announces the theft, and a spectator proposes that everyone give the same sum at the exit that he originally gave when entering. Everyone gives much more and the receipts are considerable. Typical of American generosity. Their hospitality, their cordiality are like that too, spontaneous and without affectation. It's what's best in them.

Their love of animals. Pet stores with several floors: on the first floor the canaries and on the top floor the big monkeys. Several years ago on 5th Avenue a man was arrested for driving a truck with a giraffe in it. He explained that his giraffe lacked fresh air in the suburbs where he kept it, and that this was his solution. In Central Park, a lady grazes a gazelle. In court the lady explains that the gazelle is a person.

"However, it doesn't speak," says the judge.

"Yes, the language of goodness."

Five dollar fine. After that, a tunnel 3 kilometers long under the Hudson and the terrific New Jersey bridge.

After the lecture, a drink with Schiffrin,[6] Dolores Vanetti, who speaks the purest slang that I've ever heard, and others. Mrs. Schiffrin asks me if I've ever been an actor.

• F R I D A Y.

Knopf.[7] 11 A.M. The big time. 12. Broadcasting. Gilson is nice. We'll go see the Bowery together. I have lunch with Rube and J. de Lannux who takes us for a drive through New York. Beautiful blue sky which forces me to remember that we're on the same latitude as Lisbon, something which is hard to believe. In rhythm with the traffic, the gilded skyscrapers turn and turn in the blue above our heads. It's a good moment.

We go to Tryon Park above Harlem and look down at the Bronx on one side, the Hudson on the other. Brilliant magnolias all over the place. I sample a new specimen of these "ice creams" which are such a joy to me. Another good moment.

At 4 o'clock Bromley is waiting for me at the hotel. We take off for New Jersey. Gigantic landscape of factories, bridges, and railroads. And then, suddenly East Orange and a countryside as postcard as can be, with thousands of neat and tidy cottages like toys in the midst of tall poplars and magnolias. I'm shown the little public library, bright and gay, which the neighborhood uses a lot —with a huge room for children. (Finally a country where the children are really taken care of.) I look in the card catalogue under philosophy: W. James and that's it.

At Bromley's house, American hospitality (in fact, his father is from Germany). We work on the translation of *Caligula*, which he has finished. He explains to me that I don't know how to take care of my publicity, that I have a standing here of which I should take advantage, and that the success of *Caligula* here would put me and my children on Easy Street. By his calculations I should make 1,500,000 dollars. I laugh and he shakes his head. "Aach! You don't have any *sense*." By the time we return to the city, we've become quite friendly. He's a great guy and he wants us to go to Mexico together. (*N.B.*: he's an American who doesn't drink!)

• SATURDAY.

Régine. I bring her my presents and she cries tears of gratitude!

A drink at Dolores'. Then Regine takes me on a tour of the big American department stores. I think of France. In the evening dinner with L.M. From the top of the Plaza, I admire the island covered with its stone monsters. In the night with its millions of lit windows, and its large black walls which carry the flickering lights halfway into the sky, I have the impression that a gigantic fire is under way which would raise to the horizon thousands of immense black carcasses stuffed with tiny points of combustion. The charming countess.

• SUNDAY.

A trip to Staten Island with Chiaromonte and Abel.[8] On the way back, in lower Manhattan, an immense geological dig between skyscrapers which stand very close to one another; we advance, overwhelmed by a feeling of something prehistoric. We eat in Chinatown. And I breathe for the first time in a place where I feel the expansive but orderly life that I truly love.

• MONDAY MORNING.

Walk with Georgette Pope who came to my hotel, God knows why. She's from New Caledonia. "What is your husband's job?—Magician!" From the top of the Empire State Building, in a freezing wind, we admire New York, its ancient rivers and its overflowing of stone.

At lunch Saint-Ex.'s wife—a maniac—tells us that in San Salvador her father had, along with 17 legitimate children, forty bastards, each of whom received an acre of land.

Evening, an interview at L'Ecole Libre des Hautes Etudes. Tired, I go to Broadway with J.S.

Roller skating. W. 52nd Street. An immense rink covered with dust and red velvet. In a rectangular box stuck in the back under the ceiling, an old lady plays a great variety of tunes on a large organ. Hundreds of sailors, and girls dressed for the occasion in jumpsuits revolve arm in arm in an infernal din of little metal wheels and organ stops. The description is worth working on.

Then Eddy and Leon, a nightclub without any charm. To make up for the dreariness of the place, J.S. and I have ourselves photographed as Adam and Eve by means of two completely naked cardboard mannequins (like the ones at a fair) with holes at head level where you insert your face.

J., who has interesting things to say about American love, wants to introduce me to the taxi girls. A small, dusty, softly lit hall. Each dime buys you a dance. But if you want to talk to one of the girls, you have to go to the back of the hall where, each on one side of a small barrier, it's impossible to come any closer. Impression of repression and terrible sexual exasperation. J. tells me about V-E Day and the orgiastic scenes at Times Square.

• TUESDAY.

With Harold (charming), who also talks to me about the American woman. In the evening French Institute boring. But we go to a Negro night club with Dr. Jerry Winter. Rocco, the best Negro pianist I've heard in years. A piano on rollers which he pushes in front of him as he plays. The rhythm, force, and precision of his playing and him, jumping, dancing, throwing his head and hair right and left.

Impression that only the Negroes give life, passion, and nostalgia to this country which, in their own way, they colonized.

Night on the Bowery. Poverty—and a European wants to say: "Finally, reality." The utterly derelict. And twenty cent hotels. Decorated like a "saloon," Bowery Follies, where some very old female singers perform for an impoverished audience. And, several steps away, the most splendid bridal shops that one can imagine—everything in one place—mirrors, brilliant, etc. Yes, an astonishing night.

W. Frank.[9] One of the few superior men that I've met here. He despairs a little for the America of today and compares it with the America of the 19th century. "The great minds (Melville) have always been solitary here."

Vassar College. An army of young starlets who recline on the lawns with their long legs crossed. What they do for young people here is worth remembering.

• S U N D A Y.

Long conversation with Ch. Can we create a secular church?

The afternoon with students. They don't feel the real problem; however, their nostalgia is evident. In this country where *everything* is done to prove that life isn't tragic, they feel something is missing. This great effort is pathetic, but one must reject the tragic *after* having looked at it, not before.

• M O N D A Y.

Ryder[10] and Figari.[11] Two very great painters. Ryder's paintings, mystical in inspiration and almost workmanlike in technique (they're almost enamels) force you to think of Melville, with whom he was more or less contemporary (younger). Yes, the great America is there. And now? Figari has everything: nostalgia, strength, humor.

Then Alfred Stieglitz, a kind of old American Socrates. "As I get older, life seems more and more beautiful, but living is more and more difficult. Don't hope for anything from America. Are we an end or a beginning? I think we're an end. It's a country that doesn't know love."

In the evening. Circus. Four-ring. Everyone performs at the same time. And I don't see anything.

Tucci: Human relationships are very easy here because there are no human relationships.

Everything stays on the surface. Out of respect and from laziness.

• 19 APRIL.

Another night on the Bowery. And the "elevated" —we're in the front—which speeds along five stories above the ground, and the skyscrapers spin slowly, and the machine swallows the little red and blue lights, is momentarily digested by the little stations and then takes off again towards more and more miserable neighborhoods where there are fewer and fewer cars in the streets.

Once again the Bowery Follies and the old singers who end their careers performing here. Enormous, with sweating, bloated faces—and suddenly they start prancing around and the bundles of unshapely flesh with which they are covered start bouncing up and down. "I am a bird in a gilded cage." "I ain't got no ambition." "I'm nobody's baby," etc. The less ugly ones are not popular. Either you have to be *very beautiful* or *very ugly*. Even in ugliness there's such a thing as mediocrity. And then the night. And, in an atmosphere of squalor, these Rumanians who sing and dance until they gasp for breath. Carried to the limits of an exalted world—and that unforgettable face.

When you look from upper Riverside down the highway that runs along the Hudson, the uninterrupted line of smooth-running, well-oiled cars creates a deep and distant song which is exactly the sound of the waves.

In Philadelphia, enormous gas tanks tower over little cemeteries full of flowers.

Placid evenings on the vast lawns of Washington, when the sky turns red and the grass begins to darken—a host of Negro children, shrieking with joy, playing stickball, while Americans in unbuttoned shirts, slouched on benches, having come straight from an old movie house, with their last bit of energy suck at ice creams molded into little paper cups, while squirrels come to unearth tidbits at your feet, the delicacy of which they alone appreciate. In the one hundred thousand trees of the city, a million birds greet the appearance of the first star in the still clear sky above the Washington monument, while long-legged creatures mend their way through the paths in the grass, in view of the grand monuments, offering to the sky a momentary relaxation of their imposing face and loveless gaze.

Plague: it's a world without women and thus without air.

The one who is right is the one who has never killed. So it can't be God.

I have suddenly ceased to be curious about this country. Like certain people in whom, without explanation, I suddenly lose interest (F. reproaches me for this). And I see clearly the thousand reasons one can have for being interested in this place, I would be capable of presenting its defense and its apology, I can reconstruct its beauty or its future, but my heart has simply ceased speaking and . . .

Chinese theater in Chinatown. A large, round, dusty hall. The show lasts from 6 to 11 P.M. and is watched by 1500 Chinese who eat peanuts, jabber, enter, exit, and follow the show with a kind of steady distraction. Children run around in the middle of the hall. On stage the costumed actors work alongside musicians in street clothes and suspenders who stop playing from time to time to eat a sandwich or straighten a child's trousers. Likewise, during the action, stagehands in vests and shirtsleeves enter to pick up the sword that's fallen from the hands of someone who's died, place a chair or take one away, all of which is not really necessary. From time to time through the doors that give onto the wings one sees the actors chatting or following the action as they await their cues.

As for the play, the program being in Chinese, I tried to invent the subject. But I suspect that I misinterpreted everything. Because just as a brave man is dying on stage in a very realistic fashion amidst the lamentations of his widow and his friends, and I feel completely serious, the public laughs. And when a kind of magistrate with a grating voice makes a clownish entrance, I am the only one who laughs, the rest of the audience manifesting a kind of respectful attention. A kind of butcher covered with blood kills a man. He forces a young Chinese man to carry the body. The young man is so frightened that his knees bang against each other . . .

• FROM NEW YORK TO CANADA.

Large, clean, spacious countryside with small and large white-columned houses and tall, strong trees and lawns which are never separated by fences so that it's one lawn that belongs to everyone where beautiful children and supple adolescents laugh in a life filled with good things and rich creams. Nature here contributes to the beautiful American fairy tales.

An account of an American childhood and he looks in vain for what his heart is seeking. He resigns himself.

The owl who was playing the drums at the Bowery Follies.

Two beings love each other. But they don't speak the same language. One of them speaks both languages, but the second language very imperfectly. It suffices for them to love each other. But the one who knows both languages dies. And his last words are in his native tongue which the other is unable to grasp. He searches, he searches . . .

Small inn in the heart of the Adirondacks a thousand miles from everything. Entering my room, this strange feeling: during a business trip a man arrives, without any preconceived idea, at a remote inn in the wilderness. And there, the silence of nature, the simplicity of the room, the remoteness of everything, make him decide to stay there permanently, to cut all ties with what had been his life and to send no news of himself to anyone.

New England and Maine. The region of lakes and red houses. Montreal and the two hills. A Sunday. Boredom. Boredom. The only amusing thing: the street cars which resemble, in their form and the fact that they are gilded, carnival chariots. This big country, calm and slow. One feels that it has been completely unaware of the war. In the course of a few years Europe, which was several centuries ahead in knowledge, moved several centuries ahead in moral consciousness.

Remake and recreate Greek thought as a revolt against the sacred. But not the revolt against the sacred of the romantic—which is in itself a form of the sacred—but revolt as putting the sacred in its place.[12]

The idea of messianism at the base of all fanaticism. Messianism against man. Greek thought is not historical. The values are *pre-existant. Against modern* existentialism.[13]

Plague: Tarrou makes regular visits to the Spanish dancers. Passion is his only love. Naturally a man should fight. "But if he loves only that, what's the use of fighting."

In the American newspapers: A weapon more frightening than the atomic bomb. "In certain places in the Middle Ages the black plague killed 60% of the population. We don't know if American scientists have found a way to spread it, but in China the Japanese failed. They had sown the black plague in the rice crop."

The stupendous Quebec countryside. At the point of the Diamond Cape before the immense breach of the Saint Lawrence, air, light, and water interpenetrate in infinite proportions. For the first time on this continent a real impression of beauty and true magnitude. It seems that I would have something to say about Quebec and its history of men who came to struggle in the wilderness, driven by a force that was greater than they were. But to what end? Now there are a lot of things that artistically speaking I know I could *make work*. But this no longer means anything to me. The only thing that I want to say I have been incapable of saying up until now and I will without a doubt never say it.

Do a play about bureaucracy (as stupid in America as elsewhere).[14]

Even the Salvation Army advertises here. And in their advertisements the Salvation women have red cheeks and brilliant smiles . . .

Zaharo's[15] father. Polish. Slaps an officer at fifteen. Flees. Gets to Paris during Carnival. With the little money he has, he buys confetti and sells it. Thirty years later he has an enormous fortune and a family. Completely illiterate; his son reads whatever is at hand to him. He reads him Socrates'

Apology. "You'll no longer read me any other books," says the father. "This one says everything." And ever since he always has this book read to him. He detests judges and the police.

Manhattan. Sometimes from beyond the skyscrapers, across the hundreds of thousands of high walls, the cry of a tugboat finds you in your insomnia in the middle of the night, and you remember that this desert of iron and cement is an island.[16]

The guy from the Holland Tunnel in New York or the Sumner Tunnel in Boston. All day long on a raised footbridge he counts the cars which pass endlessly in a deafening din the whole length of the violently lit tunnel which is too long for him to be able to see either one of the exits. This is the hero of a modern novel.

B. as an elevated kind of American. His psychology: ocean people love the mountains and mountain people love the sea.

Rain on New York.[17] It flows untiringly between the high cement cubes. The taxi's rapid and monotone windshield wipers sweep a water which is incessantly reborn—bizarre feeling of remoteness. Impression of being trapped in this city, that I could escape from the monoliths that surround me and run for hours without finding anything but new cement prisons, without the hope of a hill, a real tree, or a bewildered face.

B.'s father. Supreme Court judge in Hamburg. His bedside reader is the German *Chaix Indicateur* which gives the schedules of all the trains in the entire world.[18] He knows it almost by heart, and B. cites this anomaly with an admiration absolutely devoid of irony.

New York rains. Incessant, sweeping everything. And the skyscrapers in the grey haze rise up whitened like the immense sepulchers of this city inhabited by the dead. Through the rain one sees the sepulchers sway on their foundations.

Terrible feeling of being abandoned. Even if I hugged all the beings of the world to my breast, I would remain unprotected.

Plague: To Tarrou:—Do you believe that you know life totally?

Tarrou:—Yes.

Revolt. Thorough analysis of the Terror and its relationship to bureaucracy.—Note that our age marks the end of ideologies. The atom bomb prohibits ideologies.[19]

Julian Green wonders (Journal) if it is possible to imagine a saint who writes a novel. Naturally not because there is no novel without revolt. Or one must imagine a novel which is an accusation of earthly things and man—a novel absolutely without love. Impossible.

• A T S E A.

Slowness of this return voyage. The evenings at sea and this passage from the setting sun to the moon are the only moments when I feel my heart a little relaxed. I will have always loved the sea. It will have always made everything peaceful inside me.

Terrible mediocrity of these people. Up until now I haven't suffered once from the mediocrity that may have surrounded me. Up until now. But here, this intimacy is unbearable. And at the same time, in everything this something that could go very far, if only . . .

Two young, beautiful creatures have started a romance on this boat and immediately a kind of nasty circle has closed around them. These beginnings of love! I love and approve of them from the bottom of my heart—with even a feeling of gratitude for those who preserve on this deck, in the middle of the sun-glittering Atlantic, halfway between two insane continents, these truths which are youth and love.

But why not also give this name to the longing that I feel in my heart and to the tumultuous desire to find again the impatient heart that I had at 20. But I know the remedy: I'll gaze for a long time at the sea.

Sad to still feel so vulnerable. In 25 years I'll be 57. 25 years then to create a body of work and to find what I'm looking for. After that, old age and death. I know what is the most important for me. And I still find a way to give in to little temptations, wasting time on frivolous conversations or fruitless idling about. I've mastered two or three things in myself. But how far I am from the kind of superiority that I so badly need.

Marvelous night on the Atlantic. This hour when the sun has disappeared and the moon has just barely been born, when the west is still luminous and the east is already dark. Yes, I've loved the sea very much—this calm immensity—these wakes folded under wakes—these liquid routes. For the first time a horizon that measures up to the breath of a man, a space as large as his audacity. I've always been torn between my appetite for people, the vanity and the agitation, and the desire to make myself the equal of these seas of forgetfulness, these unlimited silences that are like the enchantment of death. I have a taste for worldly vanities, my fellows, for faces but, out of step with this century, I have an example in myself which is the sea and anything in this world which resembles it. O sweetness of nights where all the stars sway and slide above the masts, and this silence in myself, this silence which finally frees me from everything.

South America

June - August, 1949.

• 30 JUNE

At sea. Exhausting day. R. and I drive full speed to
reach Marseille on time. Desdemona[1] comes
through. In Marseille, torrid heat and, at the same
time, a wind that'll blow your head off. Even nature is an enemy. Cabin to myself. I wait for the
departure, walking the decks and corridors. Feeling of shame, seeing the 4th class passengers
lodged in the hold on bunks stacked one on top of
the other, concentration camp style. Dirty diapers

hanging. Some children are going to live for 20 days in this hell. And me . . . The ship lifts anchor 2 hours late. Dinner. At my table G., Professor of History and Philosophy at the Sorbonne—a small young man who's going to meet his family in Argentina, and Mme. C. who's going to meet her husband. She's from Marseille, a tall brunette. She says anything that comes into her head—and sometimes it's amusing. Other times . . . At any rate, she's alive. The others are dead—and me too, after all. After dinner, G., who has made allusions to the condition of the plague-stricken, introduces me to a Brazilian professor and his wife as "the author of *The Plague*." I look healthy! In the "music hall" (where they could have easily accommodated half of the 4th class emigrants), G. entertains us with doodles on the shipboard piano which seems to have shot all its rods. Then a conversation. Eulogy of Salazar by the Brazilian professor. Mme. C. makes two enormous blunders trying to persuade the Brazilians that there's a revolution every day in South America. I overhear "She was from the working-class, about as low as you can get," and other gems. I say goodbye and leave. In the stern, where I take refuge, the emigrants are drinking wine from a goatskin and singing. I stay with them, unknown and happy (for ten seconds). Then I go look at the sea. A sliver of moon rises above the masts. As far as one can see, in the not yet opaque night, the sea—and a feeling of calm, a powerful melancholy rises in this moment from the waters. I've always been calm at sea, and for a moment this infinite solitude is good for me, although today I have the impression that this sea is made of all the tears in the world. I return to my cabin to write this—as I would like to do every evening, saying nothing intimate, but forgetting nothing of the day's events. Turned towards what I have left, my heart anxious, I would nonetheless like to sleep.

• JULY 1ST

Waking up with a fever, I stay in bed, dreaming and dozing for part of the morning. At 11 I feel better and go out. G. on the deck. We talk about philosophy. He wants to do the philosophy of the history of philosophy. He's dead right. But according to him, he's remained young and loves to live. He's right again. Lunch with my three musketeers. Mme. C. blunders again, asking G. if he's a high school teacher, when in fact he's a professor at the Sorbonne. But she doesn't realize it. I notice the attitude that men have towards her. They think she's superficial because she's merry. Naturally, this is an error. In the afternoon I read an account of the Brazilian revolutions—Europe is nothing. At five o'clock I go work in the sun. The sun crushes the sea, which hardly breathes, and from bow to stern the boat is full of silent people. In revenge the boat's loudspeaker blasts banalities to the four corners of the earth. I am introduced to a young Rumanian woman who's left England to go live in Argentina. A passionate one—neither beautiful nor ugly, and a light mustache. I go read in my cabin, then get dressed for dinner. Sad. I drink wine. After dinner, conversation, but I look at the sea and try once again to fix the image that I've been seeking for twenty years for these patterns and drawings made on the sea by the water thrown up by the stem.[2] When I find it, it'll be finished.

Twice, the idea of suicide. The second time, still looking at the sea, I feel a dreadful burning in my temples. I think I understand now *how* one kills oneself. Conversation again—a lot of words, not much said. In the darkness I climb to the upper deck, and, after having made some decisions about work, finish the day facing the sea, the moon, and the stars. The surface of the waters are slightly illuminated, but you feel their profound darkness. That's the way the sea is, and that's why I love it! A call to life and an invitation to death.

• J U L Y 2

Monotony settles in. A little work this morning. Sun on the upper deck. Before lunch I end up being introduced to all the passengers. We're not spoiled by a surplus of pretty women, but I say it without bitterness. The sea suddenly calm, we spend all afternoon in front of Gibraltar, this enormous rock with cement inclines and an abstract, hostile gullet. Then Tangiers with its soft white houses. At six o'clock, as the day ends, the sea rises a little and while the loudspeakers blast the *Eroica*, we leave the haughty limits of Spain and leave Europe for good. I can't stop looking at the land, my heart oppressed.

After dinner, a film. A high-powered American dud. I can only stomach the first few images. I return to the sea.

• J U L Y 3

These days are relentless. This morning a swim in the pool (the water comes up to my stomach) and ping-pong where I finally manage to stretch my muscles. This afternoon horse racing (with dice) and my usual bad luck. We're on the Atlantic, the sea is high and the boat rolls a lot. Tried to work but without much success. Finally, I read Vigny's diaries where many things enchant me, but not the side of him that's like a constipated swan. And above all I prefer this neat little cabin, this hard bunk, and this destitution. Either this stripped-down solitude or the storm of love—nothing else in the world interests me. Have I forgotten anything? I don't think so. As usual I finish the day before the sea, sumptuous this evening beneath the moon, which writes Arab symbols with phosphorescent streaks on the slow swells. There is no end to the sky and the waters. How well they accompany sadness!

• J U L Y 4

Same day. Made worse by drowsiness—as if this long series of insomniac nights were suddenly catching up with me. Several times during the day I lie down and fall asleep even though last night was a good one. Meanwhile, work, pool, sun (at 2 A.M. because the rest of the time it's a frog pond) and Vigny. I find lots of things in it which coincide with my state of mind. And this again: "If suicide is permitted, it's in one of those situations where, in the midst of a family, a man is unwanted, and his death will bring peace to those for whom his life is nothing but a problem." I must say, however, that tanned, rested, well-fed, and dressed in white, I possess all the signs of life. It seems to me that I could be attractive. But to whom?

In front of the sea, before going to bed. This time the moon lights up a corridor of sea which, with the movement of the ship, seems, in the dark ocean, to be an abundant and milky river descending relentlessly towards us.[3] During the day I have already tried to jot down some aspects of the sea:

Morning sea: Immense fish pond—heavy and wriggling—scaly—sticky—covered with cool dribble.[4]

Noon sea: pale—large iron plate turning white —greying also—it's going to turn over abruptly to offer the sun its humid side, now in the obscure shadows . . . etc.[5]

Good night.

• JULY 5

Morning some swimming, some sun, and then some work. At noon we pass the Tropic of Cancer beneath a vertical sun that kills every shadow. However, it's not excessively hot. But the sky is full of a nasty haze and the sun looks like a sickness. The sea looks like an enormous swelling with the metallic brilliance of decay. In the afternoon, a great event: we pass a ship that's following the same route we are. The greeting that the two ships give each other with three grand prehistoric animal roars, the waving of the passengers lost at sea and alert to the presence of other human beings, the irrevocable separation on the green, malevolent waters—all that weighs on the heart a little. Afterwards I remain staring at the sea for a long time, full of a strange and good exaltation. After dinner I go to the bow. The emigrants play the accordion and dance in the night, where the heat seems to mount as if it were day.

• JULY 6

The day rises on a steely sea, stormy, and full of blinding flakes of light. The sky is white with haze and heat, a dead but unbearable brilliance, as if the sun had been liquified and spread out in the thickness of the clouds over the whole expanse of the celestial skullcap. As the day advances, the heat builds in the livid air. All day long the stem flushes out swarms of flying fish from their wave bushes. At 7 in the evening the coast appears, gloomy and leprous. We disembark into the night at Dakar. Two or three cafes violently lit with neon, the tall, admirably dignified and elegant Negroes in their long white robes, the Negresses in brightly colored, traditional dresses, the smell of peanuts and dung, dust and heat. Only a few hours, but I find once again the odor of my Africa, an odor of misery and abandon, a virgin but also strong odor whose seductiveness I know. When I get back on board the boat, a letter. For the first time I go to bed slightly pacified.

• JULY 7

Night of insomnia. Heat. Swimming pool and then I come back and stretch out in my cabin. Vigny, which I finish. After breakfast I try in vain to sleep. I work until 6 with good results. And then I follow—on the deck—this strange character that I have observed since the beginning of the voyage. Even in the Tropics always dressed in a dark grey suit, stiff collar, peaked cap, black shoes, 60 years old. Small, thin, looks like a self-willed rat. Alone in the dining room, his lounge chair always in the same place on the deck, he reads nothing but *Les Nouvelles litteraires* of which he seems to have an inexhaustible supply and which he reads from beginning to end. He smokes cigar after cigar and speaks to no one. The only conversation that I've heard him have was with a sailor whom he asked whether porpoises were fat or lean. Sometimes it also happens that he'll drink (pastis) with a young German-speaking Swiss who doesn't speak French. And he doesn't speak German. This makes for a conversation of deaf-mutes. This evening, while I walked around the deck four times, I noticed that not once did he look at the sea. No one on board knows what kind of work he does.

Before dinner, I watch the sun go down. But it is absorbed by the haze well before reaching the horizon. At this moment the sea is pink on the port side and blue starboard. We proceed through a limitless expanse. There won't be any land before Rio. Suddenly the evening hour is marvelous. The thick water looks slightly tarnished. The sky expands. And then during the hour when the tranquillity is greatest, hundreds of porpoises spring out of the water, prance about for a moment, and flee towards a horizon without men. Once they've gone, it's silence and the anguish of the primitive seas. After dinner, I come back to face the sea at the bow of the boat. It's sumptuous, heavy and embroidered. The wind whips my face brutally, coming at me head on, after traversing spaces the extent of which I can't even imagine. I feel alone and a little lost, finally delighted and feeling little by little the rebirth of my strength in the face of this unknown future and this immensity which I love.

• JULY 8

Night of insomnia. All day long I have a hollow head and an empty heart. The sea is rough. The

sky is covered. The decks are deserted. Since
Dakar, there are only twenty passengers left. Too
tired to describe the sea today.

• JULY 9

Better night. In the morning I stroll on the big
empty decks. The trade winds that we run into
now have made it cooler. A short and sturdy wind
brushes the sea which twists upwards in small,
foamless waves.

A little work, a lot of idling about. I notice
that I'm not writing down conversations with the
passengers. Even though some of them—with
Delamain, the publisher, and his wife—are interesting. Read a charming novel about fidelity by
him. I'll get back to it. But it's also that my interest
at this moment is not really directed towards people but towards the sea and this profound sadness
in myself to which I am not accustomed.

At 6 P.M., at sunset, this evening as always, rec-
ords of great music. Suddenly the Toccata, just at
the moment when the sun disappears behind the
clouds accumulated on the line of the horizon. In
the operatic sky, immense red trails, black plush,
fragile architectures, which seem to be made of
wire and feathers, are set in a vast arrangement of

reds, greens, and blacks—covering the whole sky, evolving in an always changing light, following the most majestic choreography. The Toccata, on this sleeping sea, beneath the festivals of this royal sky . . . the moment is unforgettable. To such an extent that the entire ship grows quiet, the passengers crowded against the western railing of the deck, recalled to silence and to that which is most real in them, removed for a moment from the poverty of days and the pain of being.

• JULY 10

We pass the equator in the morning, in Parisian weather—cool, a little harsh, a fleecy sky, the sea slightly ruffled. The equator ceremony having been cancelled for lack of passengers, we replace the ritual with several water games in the swimming pool. And then a moment with the emigrants who are playing the accordion and singing in the bow of the ship, turned towards the desolate sea. Once more I notice amongst them a woman whose hair is turning grey, a woman of superb class, a soft, proud, and beautiful face, hands and wrists like stems, and an unequaled sense of style. Always followed by her husband, a tall, blond, taciturn man. Information gathered—she's fleeing Poland and the Russians and is seeking exile in South America. She is poor. But looking at her, I think of the well-dressed but vulgar matrons who occupy several of the first-class cabins. I still haven't dared to speak to her.

Calm day. Except for a big champagne dinner in honor of passing the equator. If there are more than four people, social gatherings are hard for me to stomach. A story of Mme. C.'s: Her grandmother: "As for me, in my life, you see, I've only skimmed over the surface of things." Her grandfather: "Come now, my dear, you've nonetheless borne me two sons!"

After dinner we passengers are treated to a Laurel and Hardy. But I flee to the bow to contemplate the moon and the Southern Cross towards which we ceaselessly advance. Surprised to see how few stars, and those almost anemic-looking, in this southern sky. I think of our Algerian nights, swarming with stars.

Stayed a long time looking at the sea. Despite all my efforts and reasonings, impossible to shake this sadness which I do not understand at all.

• JULY 11

Day breaks in the middle of the Pot au Noir[6] beneath a driving rain. The rain pours in buckets

over the decks, but the temperature remains stifling, deadly. In the middle of the day the sky
clears, but the sea is rough and the ship pitches
and rolls. Some people don't make it to the dining
room. Worked. Badly. Little by little towards evening the sky clouds up again, thickens from minute to minute. Night descends, very quickly, onto
an ink-black sea.

• JULY 12

Rain, wind, furious sea. Some people are sick. The
ship advances surrounded by the smoky sea-spray.
Slept and worked. Towards the end of the afternoon the sun appears. We're already at the latitude of Pernambouc and heading towards the
coast. In the evening the sky is overcast again.
Tragic skies come to greet us from the continent
—messengers from a dreadful shore. It's an idea
that comes to me suddenly, reawakening the ab-
surd apprehension that I had before setting out on
this trip. But a little sun will clear up everything.

• JULY 13

A radiant sun floods the spaces of the sea. And the
entire boat is bathed in a dazzling light. Swimming
pool, sun. And I work all afternoon. The evening

is cool and sweet. We arrive in two days. All of a sudden the idea of leaving this ship—this narrow cabin where during long days I was able to shelter a heart cut off from everything, this sea which has been such a help to me—frightens me a little. To begin living again, speaking. People, faces, a role to play. I'll need more courage than I feel capable of. Fortunately, I'm in good shape physically. There are moments, however, when I would like to avoid other human beings.

Late at night, on the sleeping boat, I watch the night. The curious austral moon, with its flattened summit, lights up the waters towards the south. One imagines the thousands of kilometers, these solitudes where the thick and brilliant waters are like oily fields. This at least would be peace.

• J U L Y 1 4

Endless good weather. I finish up my work, at least the work that I was able to manage on shipboard, the rest being impossible under these conditions. In the afternoon, several hundred meters away, an enormous black beast rises to the surface, rides several waves and spouts two jets of water spray. The waiter who is near me confirms that it's a whale. And without a doubt the size, the awesome power of its swimming, its aura of solitary beast . . . but I remain skeptical. In the afternoon, mail and suitcases. In the evening the Captain's reception and dinner for the 14th of July. For the first time a sunset without haze. Right and left the sun is bracketed by the first cliffs of Brazil, black facades. We dance, sign menus, exchange cards, and promise that we'll all meet again, cross our hearts. Tomorrow everyone will have forgotten everyone else. I go to bed late, tired and reasoning with myself to relax a little for my encounter with this country.

• JULY 15

At 4 A.M. a racket on the upper deck awakens me. I get up. It's still dark. But the coast is very near: black, even hills with very clear outlines, but the outlines are soft, round—old profiles of one of the oldest continents on the planet. In the distance, lights. While the darkness lifts, we follow the coast, the water quivers only slightly, we tack about and now the lights are opposite us but very distant. I return to my cabin. When I go back up, we are already in the bay, immense and smoking a little in the newborn day with the sudden condensations of light which are the islands. The mist disappears rapidly. And we see the lights of Rio running all along the coast, the "Sugar Loaf" with four lights on its summit and, on the peak of the highest of the mountains, which seem to crush the city, an enormous and unfortunate illuminated Christ. As the light gradually increases, we get a better view of the city, squeezed between the sea and the mountains, spread out lengthwise, stretched out endlessly. In the center enormous buildings. Every minute a roar above our heads: an airplane takes off in the dawning day, at first inextricably blended with the hues of the land, then rising in our direction and passing above us with its great insect buzzing. We're in the middle of the basin and the mountains make an almost perfect circle around us. Finally, a blood-red light announces the arrival of the sun, which rises up behind the eastern mountains opposite the city and begins to ascend into a pale, cool sky. The richness and sumptuousness of the colors that play on the bay, the mountains, and the sky once again induce everyone to silence. One minute later the colors seem to be the same, but it's a postcard. Nature abhors miracles that last too long.

Formalities. Then disembarking. Right away it's the whirlwind that I was afraid of. Some journalists have already come on board. Questions, photos. Neither worse nor better than anywhere else. But once in Rio, with Mme. M. and a famous Brazilian journalist—already met him in Paris, very nice—the calvary begins. In the confusion of a first day, I notice by chance:

1. They ask me to choose between a room at the embassy, which is deserted, and one of the many luxury hotels. I flee the nasty-looking hotel, and congratulate myself on finding a simple and most charming room in the completely empty embassy.

2. Brazilian drivers are either joyous madmen or icy sadists. The confusion and anarchy of this traffic are regulated by only one law: get there first, no matter what the cost.

3. There is a striking contrast between the luxurious display of palaces and modern buildings and the shanty towns, which are sometimes separated from each other by no more than a hundred yards; the shanty towns, stuck to the sides of the hills, with neither water nor light, are home to an impoverished population of both blacks and whites. The women go for water at the foot of the hills, where they wait in line, and they bring it back in pails which they carry on their heads like the women of Kabylia.[7] While they wait, an uninterrupted stream of chromed and silent beasts from the American automobile industry passes in front of them. Never have I seen wealth and poverty so insolently intertwined. It is true that, according to one of my companions, "at least they have a good time." Regret and cynicism—only B.

generous. He'll take me to the shanty towns that he knows well: "I've been a criminal reporter and a communist," he says. "Two good reasons to know the neighborhoods of misery."

4. People. Lunch with Mme. M., B., and a kind of notary, thin, cultivated and spiritual—I can only remember his unusual first name, Annibal—at a country club which perfectly resembles its name: tennis, lawns, young people. Annibal has six daughters, all of whom are pretty. He says that in Brazil the mixture of religion and love is very interesting. To a Brazilian professor who had translated Baudelaire, Annibal sent the following telegram: "Kindly retranslate me back into French immediately. Signed: Baudelaire." He resembles many of these very refined Spaniards that one meets in the Spanish provinces.

5. One of the three or four Brazilian battleships that I was shown, and that seem to me to be a little out of date, is called *Terror do Mondo*. It has seen service in several revolutions.

6. People. After lunch a reception at Mme. M's. Beautiful apartment on the bay. The afternoon is soft on the waters. A lot of people, but I forget the names. A translator of Molière who a colleague tells me added an act to *The Imaginary*

Invalid, which was not long enough to make a play out of. A Polish philosopher from whom heaven, if it is merciful, will protect me. A young French biologist on mission here, furiously appealing and nice. Above all some young people from a black theater troupe who want to put on *Caligula;* I promise to work with them. With my frightful Spanish I manage to reach an agreement with one of them who speaks Spanish: on Sunday I will go with them to a Negro ball. He's delighted with the trick we're playing on my official hosts with such a rendezvous and he keeps repeating to me: "Segreto. Segreto."

7. Just when I think everything is finished, Mme. M. announces that I'm dining with a Brazilian poet. I say nothing, promising myself that starting tomorrow I'll cut everything that isn't indispensable. And I consent with resignation. But in no way did I expect the ordeal that was to follow. Enormous, indolent, folds of flesh around his eyes, his mouth hanging open, the poet arrives. Anxieties, a sudden movement, then he spills himself into an easy chair and stays there a little while, panting. He gets up, does a pirouette and falls back down into the easy chair. He talks about Bernanos,[8] Mauriac, Brisson, Halévy.[9] Apparently he knows everybody. He's been treated badly. He's not involved in Franco-Brazilian politics, but with

some Frenchmen he created a fertilizer factory. Besides he's never been decorated. In this country they've decorated all the enemies of France. But not him, etc., etc.

He dreams for a moment, suffering visibly from God knows what, and finally surrenders the conversation to a señor who seizes hold of it greedily. Because this is a señor like the ones who walked their graceful dogs on the Calle Major in Palma, Mallorca[10] before going to watch, with the pleasure of connoisseurs, the executions of '36. He rattles on about everything: I should see this, do that, Brazil is a country where one does nothing but work, no vices, no time for them, we work, we work, and Bernanos told him, and Bernanos created in this country a way of living, ah: we love France so much . . .

Appalled by the prospect of this outing, I persuade the young biologist to come to dinner with us. In the car I ask that we not go to a deluxe restaurant. And the poet emerges from his 300 pounds and tells me, with raised finger: "There is no deluxe in Brazil. We are poor, miserable," as he affectionately taps the shoulder of the chauffeur in livery who's driving his enormous Chrysler. And having said this, the poet sighs painfully and returns to his nest of flesh where he begins distractedly gnawing at one of his complexes. The señor shows us Rio which is on the same latitude as Madagascar and oh so much more beautiful than Tananarive. "Everyone's a worker," he repeats, slouched against his cushion. But the poet stops the car in front of a pharmacy, with great effort drags himself from his seat, and asks us to kindly wait a couple of minutes for him—he's going to get an injection.

We wait, and the señor comments: "Poor fellow, he's diabetic."

"Is it getting worse?" Letarget asks politely.

Ah yes!

"It's getting worse."

The poet returns, whimpering, and collapses on his poor cushion in his miserable car. We land in a restaurant near the market—where they serve only fish—in a quadrangular, high-ceilinged room which is so brutally lit with neon that we all look like pale fish floating through unreal waters. The señor wants to order for me. But I'm exhausted and, wanting to eat lightly, I refuse everything he suggests. The poet is served first, and without waiting for us, he begins eating, sometimes using his short, fat fingers instead of his fork. He talks about Michaux,[11] Supervielle,[12] Béguin,[13] etc., stopping from time to time to spit—sitting straight up—bones and morsels of fish into his plate. It's the first time I've ever seen this operation done without the person bending over his plate. Marvelously skillful for the most part, he only misses his plate once. But then we're served, and I see that the señor has ordered fried shrimp for me, which I refuse, explaining, in what I believe to be a friendly manner, that I know this dish because it's quite common in Algeria. The señor gets angry over this. They're only trying to please me, that's all. Very humbly, in fact, very humbly. I mustn't look in Brazil for what I have in France, etc., etc. Rising up out of my fatigue a stupid anger overcomes me, and I push back from the table to get up and leave. Letarget's kind intervention and also the sympathy that I feel despite everything for this curious poet hold me back, and I make an effort to calm myself. "Ah," says the poet, sucking his fingers, "in Brazil one needs a lot of patience, a lot of patience." I simply reply, in order to get it off my chest, that it doesn't seem to me that up until now I've been lacking in patience. As quickly and as irrationally as he got excited, the señor now calms down, and to smooth things over he overpowers me with compliments that leave me speechless. All of Brazil awaits me feverishly. My visit is the most important thing that's happened in this country for many years. I'm as famous as Proust . . .

There's no stopping him now. But finally he finishes with: "It's for this reason that you should be patient with Brazil. Brazil needs your patience. Patience . . . that's what's necessary in Brazil . . ." and so on. Despite everything the rest of the meal is calm, even though the poet and the señor toss off constant asides in Portuguese, and I sense that they're complaining about me. As for the rest, these bad manners are displayed so naturally that the whole thing becomes rather friendly. Leaving the restaurant the poet declares himself in need of a cup of coffee. He drives us to his club—an imitation of an English club—where I consent to drink a "real" cognac for which I have absolutely no desire. The señor launches into an explanation of the administrative difficulties of the *Figaro*, which I already know very well, but no matter; he continues with a peremptory description which is completely false. In fact Chamfort is right: if you want to succeed in society you have to let people who don't know anything teach you a lot of things you already know. I say that I want to leave.

The señor points triumphantly at the poet, who's spread out in his easy chair behind a monstrous cigar: "S. is the greatest Brazilian poet."

To which the poet, weakly waving his cigar, replies in a pained voice: "There is no greatest Brazilian poet."

In the vestibule, just when I think it's finished, the poet suddenly becomes animated and grabs my arm. "Don't move," he says to me. "Observe with all your faculties. I'm going to show you a character from one of your novels."

We see on the sidewalk a small, thin man, fedora askew, sharp features. The poet hurries towards him, gobbles him up in a long, Brazilian hug and says to me: "This is a man. He is Deputy of the Interior. But he is a man."

The other replies that Federico is excessively kind.

The señor jumps into the game. More hugs, this time between equals, since the señor is a featherweight. And the señor pulls back the deputy's vest: "Look."

The deputy is carrying a revolver in a handsome holster. We continue on our way.

"He's killed at least 40 men," the poet says, full of admiration. "And why?—Enemies."

Ah!

"Yes, he killed one, took cover behind the cadaver, and killed the others."

"He's authorized to carry arms," Letarget says without flinching, "because he's a deputy."

Looking at me, the poet says: "Isn't he a character for you?"

"Yes," I say.

But he's mistaken—he's the one who's the character.

• JULY 16

Get up early. Work. I put my notes in order. Conversation with the waiter who's serving me. He's from Nice. He wants to go to North America because he thinks the G.I.'s are nice. Unable to obtain an immigration visa, he came to Brazil, thinking that once here it would be easier to get his visa. It's not easier. I ask him what he wants to do in the United States. He's torn between boxing and singing. For the time being he's training to be a boxer. I'll go with him Monday to his gym.

Lunch with Barleto in the home of a Brazilian woman, a novelist and translator. Charming house on the side of a hill. Naturally there are a lot of people, and among them a novelist who is said to have written the Brazilian *Buddenbrooks*, but who manifests a curious cultural ignorance. If I am to believe B., the novelist was heard to say "English authors like Shakespeare, Byron, or David Copperfield." At the same time he's obviously well-read. Since it doesn't matter to me if he mistakes David for Charles, I find him very intelligent. At lunch the Brazilian couscous turns out to be fish cakes. When I ask to see a soccer game, the guests get very excited, and when I mention that I had a long career as a soccer player, I provoke a general delirium. Unwittingly, I've stumbled upon their principal passion. But the mistress of the house translates Proust, and everyone present is profoundly knowledgeable about French culture. Afterwards I suggest to B. that we take a walk in the city.

Gaily lit up by multicolored signs, the little pedestrian streets are harbors of peace near the large arteries with their growling traffic. As if, between Concorde, the Madeleine, and the Avenue de l'Opéra, no cars were allowed on the rue St. Honoré. The flower market. Little bar where you drink "little coffees" seated on miniscule chairs. Moorish houses next to skyscrapers. Next Barleto makes me take a little tramway that climbs a steep path up the city's hills. We reach a neighborhood —at once poor and luxurious—that looks out over the city. At dusk the city extends to the horizon. Above her a multitude of colored signs stand smoking in the moist evening air. In the soft sky one can see the profiles of hills which end in jutting high palms. There is a tenderness in this sky, and a nostalgia which is almost sweet. Descending on foot, down steps and along small, slanting streets, we return to the city proper. In the first real street that we come upon, a positivist temple. There's a cult here to Clotilde de Vaux[14] and it's in Brazil that Auguste Comte is immortalized by his most disconcerting legacy. A little further on there's a Gothic church built of reinforced concrete. The temple, on the other hand, is Greek. But they must have been short of money because there are no cornices on the columns. Small bar where we chat with B.N. Charming man, sometimes profound ("by sitting in the sun and letting our skin turn dark, a certain innocence is lost") who, it seems to me, lives the drama of our era with dignity. I leave him to meet Abdias, the black actor, at Mme. Mineur's and to go on from there to a *macumba*.

• A MACUMBA, IN BRAZIL[15]

At Mme. M.'s, anxiety reigns. The "father of the saints" (priest and principal dancer), who was supposed to organize the *macumba*, consulted the saint of the day, but was refused his authorization. Abdias, the black actor, thinks he probably didn't promise enough money to win the good will of the saint. In his opinion we should risk an expedition to Caxias, a suburban village 25 miles from Rio, where by chance we might be able to find a macumba. During dinner the macumbas are explained to me. The purpose of these ceremonies is always the same: through dances and songs, to attain the descent of the god into oneself. The goal is the trance. What distinguishes macumbas from other ceremonies is the mixture of Catholicism and African rituals. There is Echou, an African god and spirit of evil, but also Ogoun who is our Saint George. There are also Saint Cosme and Saint Damien, etc., etc. The cult of saints is integrated here into rites of possession. Each day has its saint, who cannot be feted on any other day unless special authorization is obtained from the principal "father of the saints." The "father of the saints" has his daughters (and his sons, I suppose), and he is required to verify their trances.

After receiving this elementary information, we depart. 25 miles in a kind of fog. It's 10 P.M. Caxias, which makes me think of a village fair full of stands. We stop at the village square where there are already about twenty cars and many more people than we had imagined. No sooner have we stopped than a young mulatto comes up to me, offers me a bottle of aguardiente, and asks me if I've brought Tarrou with me. He breaks out laughing, jokes with me, and introduces me to his friends. He's a poet. I learn that it was known in Rio that I was to be taken to a macumba (I was told to keep it secret which I innocently did), and a lot of people have shown up. Abdias tries to get information and directions. We remain there in the middle of the square, chatting with the people from the village. Abdias is immobile. Apparently, no one is taking care of anything; everyone is just standing around, staring up at the stars. Suddenly: general excitement. Abdias tells me that we have to go up the mountain. We take off, drive several miles on a beat-up road and then, for no apparent reason, suddenly stop. Waiting—no one seems to be doing anything. Then off we go again. Suddenly the car turns a 45 degree angle and sets off up the mountain road. It struggles painfully for a few minutes and then stops: it's too steep. We leave the car behind and set off on foot. The hill is barren, very little vegetation, but we're in the open sky, amidst the stars, it seems. The air smells of smoke. It's so thick you seem to be cutting through it as you walk. At the summit of the hill we hear the drums and songs in the distance, but then they stop. We walk in their direction. No trees, no houses; it's a desert. But in a hollow we see a kind of vast hangar without walls. Paper garlands are strung across the ceiling. Suddenly I see a procession of black girls coming towards us. They're dressed in long-waisted white dresses made of coarse silk. A man is following them. He's dressed in a kind of red jumper and is wearing necklaces of multicolored teeth. Abdias stops him and introduces me. His greeting is serious, but friendly. But there is a complication. They're going to join another macumba twenty minutes away, and we have to follow them. We set out. At a crossroads I see a kind of niche where the statues of saints or devils (extremely crude, in the style of Saint Sulpice) are set in front of a candle and a bowlful of water.[16] They show me Echou, red and ferocious, with a knife in his hand. The path snakes through the hills under a star-filled sky. The dancers go on ahead of us, laughing and joking. We go down one hill, cross the road by which we arrived, and start up another hill. Cabins made of branches and clay, full of whispering shadows. Then the procession stops in front of a raised terrace surrounded by a wall of reed stalks. We hear drums and songs coming from inside. When we're all together, the first women climb up the terrace and enter backwards through the reed door. Then the men. We enter a courtyard full of rubbish. The sound of singing is coming from a little thatched house opposite us. We go in. It's a very crude kind of cabin; however, the walls are stuccoed. The roof is held up by a central mast, the floor is earthen. A small lean-to shelters an altar above which is a colored image of St. George.[17] Similar images are hung around the walls. In a corner, on a little platform decorated with palm leaves, three musicians are playing short and long drums. Before we arrived there were already some forty dancers. We double that number so it's very crowded and hard to breathe. I back up against a wall and watch. The dancers set themselves in two concentric circles, the men inside and the women outside. The two "fathers of the saints" (the one who welcomed us is dressed, like the dancers, in what looks like white pajamas) are face to face in the center of the circles. One after the other they sing the first notes of a song that's taken up in chorus by the dancers. The circles move clockwise. The dance is simple: a foot stamp onto which is grafted the double undulation of the rhumba. The "fathers" mark the rhythm very lightly. My translator informs me that the songs are entreating the saint to authorize our presence in this place. The breaks between the songs are rather long. Near the altar one woman singer shakes a small bell incessantly. The dancing is hardly frenetic. The style is mediocre and it's heavy. As it gets hotter, the breaks are almost unbearable. I notice:

1. that the dancers don't even work up a light sweat;

2. a white man and woman who dance worse than the others.

One of the dancers approaches and speaks to me. My translator tells me that I am being asked to uncross my arms because this position impedes the descent of the spirit. I submit and keep my arms at my sides. Little by little the breaks between the songs get shorter and the dance more lively. A lit candle is brought to the center and stuck in the earth near a glass of water. The songs invoke St. George.

> *He arrives in moonlight*
> *He leaves in sunlight*

and continues:

> *I am the battlefield of god.*

In fact, one or two of the dancers already seem to be in a trance, but, if I may say so, the trance is rather calm: hands on the small of the back, legs stiff, eyes unmoving and vacant.[18] The "father" in red pours water in two concentric circles around the candle, and almost without interruption the dances resume, one after the other. From time to time a man or woman leaves the circles to dance in the middle, near, but never crossing, the circles of water. Their rhythm is faster, and they're seized by spasms and inarticulate cries. The dust rises from the floor and thickens the air which is already stifling. More and more dancers leave the circles to dance around the two fathers who have also quickened the tempo of their movements (the father in white dances very well). Now the drums are raging, and all of a sudden the father in red breaks loose.[19] Eyes inflamed, arms and legs whirling around his body, he leaps from leg to leg with bent knee, accelerating his rhythm until the dance ends and he stands staring at everyone with a fixed and frightening gaze. At this moment a dancer comes forward from a dark corner, kneels, and offers him a sheathed sword. The father in red pulls the sword and swings it around his body in a threatening manner. They bring him an enormous cigar. Little by little everyone lights cigars and smokes them while they dance. The dance continues. One by one the dancers prostrate themselves before the father, placing their heads between his feet. He hits them diagonally with the flat of the sword, stands them up, touches his right shoulder to their left and vice versa. He pushes them violently into the circle, and two out of three times this movement sets off a crisis which takes a different form depending on the dancer: a fat black man, immobile, staring vacantly at the central mast, has only a quivering at the back of his neck which continues incessantly. He looks like a boxer down for the count. A thick white woman with an animal face barks relentlessly, shaking her head from right to left.[20] But the young black women enter into the most hideous trance, their feet glued to the ground and their bodies racked by starts and jerks which become more violent as they ascend toward the women's shoulders. Their heads shoot back and forth and look as if they are going to fly off their necks. They scream and howl. Then the women begin to fall. They are picked up, patted on the forehead, and they start in again until they fall once more. The summit is reached when everyone starts screaming: strange, hoarse sounds that resemble barking. I am told that this will continue incessantly until dawn. It's 2 A.M. The heat, the dust, the cigar smoke, and the smell of bodies make the air unbreathable. I go out staggering, and breathe in the fresh air with delight. I like the night and the sky better than the gods of men.

• J U L Y   1 7

Work in the morning. I eat lunch with G. and two Brazilian professors. Three professors in fact, but nice. Then Lucien Febvre,[21] an old, rather taciturn man, joins us, and we take a drive through the mountains that encircle Rio. One hundred views of the Tijuca gardens, the Meyrink chapel, the Corcovado, the bay of Rio—each view very different from all the others. And the immense beaches of the South, with white sand and emerald waves, which run deserted for thousands of miles into Uruguay. The tropical forest and its three layers. Brazil is a land without men. Everything created here is created at the price of inordinate efforts. Nature suffocates man. "Is space sufficient to create culture?" the good Brazilian professor asks me. It's a meaningless question. But these spaces are the ones that will gain from technical progress. The faster the airplane flies, the less important are France, Spain, and Italy. They were nations, now they are provinces, and tomorrow they will be the world's villages. The future is not ours, and there's nothing we can do against this irresistible movement. Germany lost the war because it was a nation and modern warfare requires the means of empires. Tomorrow the means of entire continents will be necessary. And now the two great empires seek the conquest of their continents. What's to be done? The only hope is the birth of a new culture, and a South America that can perhaps mollify the mechanical folly.[22] That's what I badly expressed to my professor as we sat before a hissing sea, letting sand run between our fingers.

After being chilled in the car and also under the Corcovado Christ, I return to the hotel to wait for the faithful Abdias who's supposed to take me to dance the samba after dinner. Disappointing evening. In an outlying neighborhood, a kind of working class dance hall lit, of course, by neon. For the most part there are only blacks, but in Brazil this means a great variety of skin colors. Surprised to see how slowly these blacks dance, as if underwater. Perhaps it's the climate. The Harlem madmen would probably calm down here. Except for the color of the skin, nothing distinguishes this dance hall from a thousand others throughout the world. Speaking of this, I notice that I have to conquer in myself a reverse prejudice. I like blacks *à priori*, and I'm tempted to see in them qualities that they don't really have. I want these people to be beautiful, but if I imagine them with white skin, I find a rather pretty collection of clerks and dyspeptic employees. Abdias agrees. The race is ugly. However, of the mulatto women who immediately come to drink at our table, not because it's ours but because we're drinking there, one or two are pretty. I'm even attracted to one who's lost her voice, dances a lax samba with another woman, taps me on the side to awaken my appetite, and then suddenly informs me that I'm bored. Taxi. I return to the hotel.

• J U L Y 1 8

It's pouring buckets onto the smoking bay and onto the city. Calm morning of work. I go to lunch with Lage in a nice restaurant that gives onto the port. I have a date with Barleto at 3 to visit the working class suburbs. We take a suburban train. *Meier. Todos os santos.*[23] *Madeidura.* I'm struck by how Arab it seems. Stores without shop-fronts. Everything is in the street. Saw a hearse: a cenotaph in Empire style with enormous gilded bronze columns on a delivery truck painted black. Let the rich have horses. Violently colored fabrics on display. We cross interminable suburbs in a bumpy streetcar. Sad and most of the time empty (the tribes of workers camped at the entrances of housing developments[24] remind me of B.[25]) but coagulating at long intervals around a center, a square brilliant with neon, with red and green lights (in the middle of the day), crammed with this multicolored crowd at whom, from time to time, a loudspeaker screams the latest football scores. One thinks of these crowds of people, incessantly growing over the surface of the world, who will eventually cover everything and end up suffocating themselves. I understand Rio better like this, at any rate better than at the Copacabana—that aspect of it that's like an oil stain extending infinitely in every direction. Returning in a *lotacao*, a kind of group taxi, we see one of the numerous accidents that result from this unbelievable traffic. On an avenue shimmering with lights a speeding bus hits a poor, old black man, sends him flying like a tennis ball, drives around the body, and takes off. The driver flees because of the stupid law of *flagrante delicto*, which would send him to prison. So he takes off, there's no *flagrante delicto*, and he won't go to prison. Nobody comes to help the old black man. The shot he took would have killed a bull. Later on I learn that they'll put a white sheet over him—which will slowly turn red with his blood—set lit candles around him, and the traffic will continue to by-pass him until the authorities arrive.

In the evening, dinner at Robert Claverie's. Nothing but French, which is relaxing. Huxley says that when one speaks a foreign language there's someone inside of oneself who refuses.

• J U L Y 1 9

Beautiful weather. A charming, myopic lady journalist. Mail. Lunch with the Delamains in a restaurant at the train station—neon, of course. The meal. Dark thoughts. At the end of the afternoon I go to a drama school. Interview with professors and students. Dinner at the Chapass' home with the national poet Manuel Bandera, a small, extremely refined man. After dinner Kaimi, a black man who writes and composes the sambas that are sung throughout Brazil, comes to sing and play his guitar. Of all songs these are the saddest and most moving. The sea and love, nostalgia for Bahia. Little by little everyone sings. One sees a black man, a deputy, a university professor, and a notary public sing these sambas together with very natural grace. Completely seduced.

• JULY 20

Beautiful morning in a motor boat on the bay of Rio. Only a light, cool wind brushes the surface of the water. We run alongside the islands; little beaches (two twins named Adam and Eve). Finally, a swim in the pure, cool water. Afternoon, a visit from Murillo Mendès—a poet and in poor health. A pure, unyielding spirit. Really one of the two or three that I've noticed here. Lecture in the evening. When I arrive, I find a crowd blocking the entrance. Unable to find a seat, Claverie and the ravishing Mme. Petitjean are about to leave. I manage to get seats for them, but not without difficulty. The auditorium holds 800 people, but it's overflowing and some of the public are obliged to stand or sit on the floor. The society people, diplomats, etc., naturally arriving late, have to choose between standing or leaving. The Spanish ambas-

sador sits behind the rostrum on a board sup-
ported by two sawhorses. In a little while he'll be
educated. Ninu, a Spanish refugee whom I knew
in Paris, is there! He's head of the *campeones* in a
ranch 60 miles from Rio. He came 60 miles to
hear his *"campañero."* He's leaving tomorrow
morning. When you know what it means to go 60
miles on these roads . . . I'm moved to tears. Taking out a pack of cigarettes, he tells me that these
are closest to the *"gusto frances,"* and offers me
one. I stick close to him all evening, happy to have
him in the auditorium and thinking to myself that
it's for men like him that I'm going to speak. And,
in fact, this is how I speak,[26] and I get through to
the men like N., and, it seems to me, to the young
people who are there. But I doubt that I win over
the society people. Afterwards, the stampede. I
harvest several honest responses. The rest is play-
acting. Go to sleep at midnight, knowing I have to
get up at 4:30 A.M. for a plane to Recife.

• J U L Y 2 1

Get up at 4 A.M. It's pouring. Just going from the
embassy door to the taxi, I get soaked. During the
formalities at the airport I'm asleep on my feet.
It's a long way from the airport to the aerodrome.
In this climate one gets wet twice: once from the
rain, and then from one's own perspiration. A

long wait. We don't end up leaving until 8:30, and once again I'm in a rage against airplanes. While I'm waiting I look at a chart that shows the distances between Rio and the capitals of the world. Paris is 6000 miles away. Two minutes later *La vie en rose* on the radio. Under a low sky, burdened with rain, the airplane takes off heavily. I try to sleep but can't. Four and a half hours later, when we land at Recife, the airplane door opens onto red earth consumed by heat. It's true that we're once again at the equator. Insomniac, vaguely feverish from a cold I've caught this morning, I stagger under the weight of the heat. No one's waiting for me. It's not surprising since it seems the plane is early. So I wait in an empty room in air that's on fire, contemplating in the distance the coconut forests that surround the city. The delegation arrives. Everybody nice. The three Frenchmen who are there are all over six feet tall. We're well represented. We take off. Red earth and coconut trees. And then the sea and immense beaches. Hotel on the pier. The masts are higher than the parapet. I try to sleep. In vain. Four hours. They come to fetch me. There's the director of the oldest newspaper in South America, *Le journal de Pernambouc.* He's the one who takes me around the city. Admirable, very white colonial churches, where the Jesuitic style is made clearer and lighter by the stucco. The interior is baroque, but without the excessive heaviness of European baroque. The Golden Chapel in particular is admirable. Here the *azulejos* are perfectly preserved. Only the "wicked" Judas, the Roman soldiers, etc. have been disfigured by the people; and it's the same thing with the paintings. All their faces are consumed and bloody. I admire the old city—the red, blue, and ochre houses, the streets paved with large pointed pebbles. The square of the San Pedro church. Right next to a coffee factory the church is black from the smoke of the roasters. It literally has a coffee patina.

Dinner alone. Faintly, the sound of an orchestra. Exile has its pleasures. After dinner, a lecture for about one hundred people who, as they leave, seem very tired. I definitely do like Recife. Florence of the tropics, between its coconut forests, its red mountains, its white beaches.

• JULY 22

Wake up with the grippe and a fever. Wobbly legs. I get dressed and wait at the hotel for three intellectuals who are determined to see me. Two are pleasant. We go to see Olinda, a small, historic city with old churches, on the bay opposite Recife. Very beautiful convent of Saint-Francis. When I return I'm shivering with fever and take aspirin and gin. Lunch at the consul's. After lunch a walk through a coconut forest that borders the sea. Through the openings we see the sails of *junsahés* at sea, a kind of narrow raft, made of trunks of a very light wood held together by rope. I'm told that these fragile assemblages can remain at sea for days and days. Here and there straw huts. But in the suffocating, luminous air, the shadow of the coconut trees trembles before my eyes. The grippe gets worse and, with an interview at 5 o'clock, I excuse myself to rest. Can't sleep. A round table discussion which, thanks to two whiskeys, I manage to get through. Afterwards, departure for a fiesta organized for me. They give me an injection for my grippe. Uninteresting songs and dances. A chic macumba. But the *bomba-men-boi* is an extraordinary spectacle. It's a kind of grotesque ballet danced by masked dancers and totem figures on a theme that never varies: the putting to death of a steer. While they dance the characters recite, and improvise, a text in verse. What I see lasts one hour. But I'm told that it can last all night. The masks are extraordinary. Two red clowns, the "sailor horseman" inside a merry-go-round horse, a swan, a clown dressed as a gaucho. Two Indians, and of course the steer—the "dead bearing the living"—a kind of two-bodied figure worn by a single actor, the *cachasa* (or drunk), the son of the horse, a prancing colt, a man on stilts, the crocodile, and, dominating everything, a dead man at least 9 feet tall who contemplates the performance, his head high up in the night sky. The orchestra consists of a drum and a steel drum. The religious origins are evident (there are still prayers in the text). But all that is drowned in a diabolic dance, a thousand graceful or grotesque inventions ending with the murder of the steer which is reborn soon afterwards and carries off a little girl between its horns. The end—a great shout: "Long live Señor Camus and the one hundred *kings* of the Orient." I return to the hotel, brutalized by the grippe.

• JULY 23

9 A.M. Leave for Bahia. My grippe is a little better. But I'm still feverish and aching. It's cold in the airplane, God knows why. And it bounces around terribly. After three hours we see the appearance of little hills covered with snow on a vast plain. At least that's the impression that this white sand, which is everywhere here, gives me, immaculate waves which resemble a desert surrounding Bahia. From the aerodrome to the city four miles of road winds between banana trees and dense vegetation. The earth is completely red. Bahia, where one sees only blacks, seems to me to be an enormous collection of markets—teeming, impoverished, filthy,

and beautiful. Innumerable stands made of torn sheets and old planks, old, low houses stuccoed with red, apple-green, and blue lime, etc.

Lunch at the port. Large boats with blue and ochre lateen sails unload bunches of bananas. We eat dishes that are spicy enough to make cripples walk again. The bay that I see from the window of my hotel extends round and pure, full of a strange silence, beneath a grey sky, while the immobile sails that one sees seem imprisoned in a sea that has suddenly become rigid. I prefer this bay to the one at Rio—too spectacular for my tastes. At least this one has moderation and poetry. Since the morning brutal and abundant downpours. They've transformed the broken streets of Bahia into rushing torrents. And we drive in the middle of two large blades of water which pour down incessantly over both sides of the car.

Visit the churches. Even though they have bigger reputations, they're the same as the ones at Recife. The Church of the Good Jesus with its votive offerings (plaster casts, a buttocks, an X-ray, corporal's stripes). Suffocating. But this harmonious baroque is very repetitive. In fact, it's the only thing to see in this country and it doesn't take long to see it. Real life remains. But in this oversized land which has the sadness of large spaces, life is terribly banal and it would take years to integrate oneself. Do I want to spend years in Brazil? No. At 6 P.M. I take a shower, sleep, and wake up feeling a bit better. Dinner alone. Then a lecture before a patient public. The consul joins me afterwards and, after the last glass has been drunk, slips me, under the table, an envelope containing approximately 45,000 francs in Brazilian currency. This is what I'm being paid by the University of Bahia. The consul's surprise when I refuse. He explains to me that "there are others who demand this payment." Finally he desists. I know that he can't help thinking: "If he needed it, he'd accept." In fact . . .

Before finishing I jot down several of the house rules in the French of the Palace(?) Hotel of Bahia—"In Brazil everyone speaks French." So goes the propaganda.

"The failure to pay bills, as stipulated in paragraphs 3 and 4, will oblige the management to effect the withholding of baggage as security against the debt, and as a consequence the client will immediately disoccupy the occupied room."

"It is prohibited to possess birds, dogs, or other animals in the rooms."

"In the hotel lobby one still finds a well-appointed American Bar and a spacious reading room."

And this one for the end:

"In the hotel lobby there is a barber shop and a manicure salon. The clients can employ their functions in their rooms."

• J U L Y 2 4 (S U N D A Y)

At 10 A.M. Eduardo Catalao, a charming Brazilian who is polite in a way that people no longer are, takes me, by way of a road in extreme disrepair, to the Itapoa beach. It's a village of fishermen in straw huts. But the beach is wild and beautiful, the sea frothy at the foot of the coconut trees. This grippe, which won't end and has me enslaved, keeps me from going swimming. We meet a group of young French film people who are living in a straw hut and making a film about Bahia. Surprised to see me in this out of the way place. They smell a little of St.-Germain-des-Prés.

A vitriolic lunch at three. From 5 to 7, I work. Dinner at the consul's. Then we go to see a *candomble*,[27] a new ceremony of this curious Afro-Brazilian religion which is the Catholicism of the blacks here. It's a kind of dance executed in front of a food-laden table, accompanied by three drums of different sizes and a flattened funnel that is struck with a thin, iron stick. The dances are directed by a kind of matron (who replaces the "fathers of the saints") and all the dancers are women. The costumes are much richer than at Bahia. Two of the dancers, both enormous, have their faces covered by straw veils. Nonetheless I learn nothing new until the entrance of a group of young black girls, semi-hypnotized, eyes almost closed, standing straight but swinging their feet forward and back. One of them, a tall thin girl, delights me. She's wearing a green dress and a blue huntress' hat with musketeer feathers and the brim turned up. In her hand she's holding a green and yellow bow loaded with an arrow at the end of which is a brooch representing a multicolored bird. The handsome, sleeping face reflects a smooth and innocent melancholy. This black Diana is infinitely graceful. And when she dances, this extraordinary gracefulness remains undiminished. When the music stops, she totters. The rhythm alone lends her a kind of invisible guardian around which she spins her arabesques, uttering from time to time a strange, piercing but somehow melodious bird cry. All the rest isn't worth much. Mediocre dances expressing degenerated rituals. We leave with Catalao. But in this faraway neighborhood, as we stumble along the streets full of holes, through the heavy, aromatic night, the wounded bird's cry comes back to me and I recall my beautiful slumbering one.

I would like to go to bed, but Catalao wants to drink whiskey in one of those morbidly depressing night clubs one can find anywhere. Without my knowing, he requests some French music and, for the second time, I hear *La vie en rose* in the Tropics.

• JULY 25

Wake up at 7 A.M. I have to wait for an airplane that may or may not leave. Then it's confirmed. It will depart at 11 A.M. My grippe is better, but my legs are shaky. Furious desire to return home. I lose two hours at the aerodrome. We leave. It's 1:30 and we won't arrive in Rio before 7. I'm writing all this in the airplane, where I feel very alone.

Evening. Arrived with a furious relapse into both grippe and fever. This time it seems serious.

• J U L Y 2 6

In bed. Fever. Only the mind works on, obstinately. Hideous thoughts. Unbearable feeling of
advancing step by step toward an unknown catas-
trophe which will destroy everything around me
and in me.

Evening. They come to fetch me. I'd forgotten that tonight the black theater group was supposed to show me an act of *Caligula*. The theater's
been reserved and there's nothing to be done. I
cover myself as if I were going to the North Pole
and take a taxi.

Strange to see these black Romans. And then
what seemed to me to be a cruel and vigorous text
has become a slow, tender, vaguely sensual cooing.
After that they perform a short Brazilian play
which I enjoy very much. Here's a synopsis:

"A man who frequently participates in macumbas is visited by the spirit of love. He showers
attentions on his wife, who is transported and falls
in love with the spirit inhabiting her husband.
With the same song, as often as possible, she in-
vokes the presence of the spirit, which on stage
becomes a pretext for frequent and animated bac-
chanals. Finally the husband understands that she
is in love not with him but with God, and he kills

her. She dies happily, however, because she's convinced that she's going to join her beloved God."

The evening ends with Brazilian music which seems, to me, mediocre. Important, however, that Brazil is the only country with a black population that continually produces new tunes. The finale is a frevo, a dance from Pernambouc, in which everyone participates and which is the wildest contortion that I've seen so far. Charming. As soon as my head hits the pillow, I'm out like a light, and I don't wake up until 9 A.M., infinitely better.

• JULY 27

Set on this immense continent teeming with natural and primitive forces, Brazil, with its thin armor of modernity, makes me think of a building being gnawed at by invisible termites. One day the building will collapse, and a swarm of little people— black, red, and yellow—will spread across the surface of the continent, masked and armed with spears, for the victory dance.

Breakfast with the poet Murillo Mendès (a sensitive and melancholy spirit), his wife, and a young poet whom Rio's intelligent traffic system cost 17 fractures and a pair of crutches. After breakfast they take me to the "Sugar Loaf." But the morning is spent waiting in line, and we never get past the first peak—to the great distress of Mme. Mendès who's sure I'm bored when in fact I'm in a good mood because their company is so pleasant. M. knows and quotes Char[28] and believes that he's our most important poet since Rimbaud. That makes me happy.

• JULY 28

The Montevideo embassy complicates my stay by wanting to change the dates that had been agreed upon. Finally, it's agreed I'll stay in Rio until Wednesday before going to São Paulo. Lunch with Simon and Barleto whom I like more and more each day. The afternoon spent working. In the evening a charming reception at the embassy, but I'm bored there. I take French leave, as they say here, and go home to bed.

• JULY 29

The days in Rio hardly make any sense and pass quickly and, at the same time, slowly. Lunch with Mme. B. and her sister-in-law. French women have their good sides. Lively, spiritual; the time passes quickly. Then a walk along the bay in marvelous, soft weather. With difficulty I tear myself away from these pleasant, natural moments to run off to the embassy to meet Mendès and his wife who are supposed to take me to Correa's, an ex-publisher, where I'm to meet a student who . . . , etc. What I've obstinately refused all my life, I accept here—as if in advance I had agreed to everything about this trip which I never wanted to undertake in the first place. I leave in time to meet Claverie, Mme. B., and her sister-in-law, whom I've invited to dinner. After dinner Claverie drives us along roads which bore through the mountain and the night. The warm air, the tiny, numerous stars, the bay below . . . but all this makes me more melancholy than happy.

• JULY 30 AND 31

Weekend at Cl.'s in Térésopolis. In the mountains 90 miles from Rio. The drive is beautiful, especially between Pétropolis and Térésopolis. From time to time you round a corner and an ipecac bush covered with yellow flowers bursts upon you against a background of mountains which extend to the horizon. One again understands here what had struck me when I was in an airplane flying over this country. Immense, virgin, and solitary expanses in the face of which the cities, set along the shore, are no more than little specks of no importance. At any moment this enormous conti-

nent, entirely surrendered to the natural wilderness, could turn upon and cover over the false
luxuriousness of these cities. The weekend is spent
taking walks, swimming, and playing ping-pong. In
this countryside I can finally breathe. And the air
at 2600 feet shows me how exhausting the climate
of Rio really is. When we go back down Sunday
night, it's without pleasure that I return to the
city. Besides, in front of the embassy, I'm welcomed back by one of those scenes too frequently
witnessed in Rio. Once again, a bleeding woman
stretched out in front of a bus. And a crowd looking on in silence without helping her. This barbarian practice disgusts me. Much later I hear the si-
ren of an arriving ambulance. During all that time
the poor, dying woman was left moaning in the
street. As compensation they make a big show of
adoring children.

• A U G U S T 1

Difficult waking. To live is to hurt others, and
through others, to hurt oneself. Cruel earth! How
can we manage not to touch anything? To find
what ultimate exile?

Lunch at the embassy. I learn that in Brazil
there is no death penalty. In the afternoon a lecture on Chamfort.[29] I wonder why I always attract

worldly women. A lot of fancy hats! Dinner with
Barleto, Machado, etc. in a nice Italian restaurant.
In the afternoon we go to a suburban ghetto. Numerous negotiations before entering this "city" of
wood, tin, and reeds, stuck to the flank of a hill
above the Ipanema beach. Finally, we're told that
we can have a consultation (it's true that we have
as a letter of introduction two good bottles of
cachado) with one of the ladies of the place. It's
night when we enter, passing between compart-
ments where the sound of radios and snoring can
be heard. The ground is slippery, covered with
garbage, and sometimes absolutely vertical. It
takes us a good fifteen minutes to arrive, out of
breath, at the pythoness' hut. But on the terrace,
in front of the hut, we're rewarded: beneath a
half-moon the motionless beach and bay are
stretched out before us. The pythoness seems to
be sleeping. But she lets us in. I've seen a lot of
huts like this, with multicolored fabrics hanging
from the ceiling. In a corner a bed with someone
sleeping on it. In the middle a table with laundry
covered by a red curtain that makes it look like a
cadaver. An alcove where there's an altar and all
the statues of saints that St. Sulpice exports
throughout the world. Also a statue of *Redskin*—
how it got there is anyone's guess. The pythoness
gives the impression of being a nice, honest home-
maker. She's just finished her consultations, which

she gives only when the saint is within her. The saint has left. We'll have to come back another time. It's hot. But these blacks are so nice and pre-possessing that we stay and chat. Descending is a real race with death. One imagines the women going to get water two or three times a day, and climbing back up with the bucket on their heads. One imagines the days when it's raining. As it is, Barleto takes a spill. I arrive safe and sound, and the evening ends at the home of Machado, who tells me about the healers who help the dying in Minas.[30] In certain cases, when the agony lasts too long, these men, who are licensed, are called. They arrive, dressed as masters of ceremony, say hello, take off their gloves and go to the dying one. They have him repeat "Mary-Jesus" without stopping, place a knee on his stomach, cover his mouth and apply pressure until their agonized client has crossed to the other side. They retire from the room, put their gloves back on, receive fifty cruzeiros and leave, accompanied by the grat-itude and esteem of the dead man's family.

• AUGUST 2

Tired of writing down meaningless bits and pieces. (I'm writing this in the airplane that's taking me to São Paulo. Yesterday was full of meaningless bits and pieces. Even a conversation with Mendès on the relationship between culture and violence, which helped me clarify my thoughts, seemed meaningless to me.)

In reality, haunted in the glorious light of Rio by the idea of the harm we do to others from the moment we look at them. I have to confess that for a long time making people suffer was a matter of indifference to me. It's love that enlightened me on this point. Now I can no longer bear it. In a way it's better to kill someone than to make him suffer.

What I realized clearly yesterday is that I want to die.

• AUGUST 3

São Paulo and the sun setting fast—bright signs light up one by one on top of the massive skyscrapers. Royal palm trees rise up between the buildings and the uninterrupted song of thousands of birds, welcoming the day's end, is heard, muffling the low-pitched car horns which announce the return of the businessmen. Dinner with Oswald de Andrade, remarkable character (develop this). His point of view is that Brazil is populated with primitive people and that it's for the best.

The city of São Paulo, strange city, limitless Oran.

Stupidly I forgot to note the thing which touched me the most. On São Paulo radio there's a program in which poor people go on the air to speak of their problems and ask for help. This evening a large, poorly dressed black man with a little girl of 5 months in his arms and the baby's bottle in his pocket explained frankly and simply that since his wife had abandoned him, he was looking for someone who would take care of the child without stealing her from him. An ex-fighter pilot, unemployed, was looking for a job as a mechanic, etc. Then, in the offices, we wait for telephone calls from the listeners. Five minutes after the end of the program, the phone is ringing constantly. Everybody offers something. While the black man is on the phone, the ex-pilot rocks the infant in his arms. And here's the best one: a large, older black man, half-dressed, comes into the offices. He was sleeping and his wife, who was listening to the program, woke him up and said: "Go get the child."

• AUGUST 4

Press conference in the morning. Lunch standing up at Andrade's. I don't really know why, but at 3 o'clock, I'm taken to the city penitentiary, "the most beautiful one in Brazil."[31] In fact, it is beautiful, like a penitentiary in an American film. Except for the odor, the hideous odor of man that lingers in every prison. Iron bars, doors, bars, doors, etc. And the signs. "Be good" and above all "Optimism." I feel ashamed in front of one or two of the prisoners—and these are ones with special privileges—who have service jobs in the prison. Then the doctor-psychiatrist treats me to an interminable dissertation on the classification of perverse mentalities. And as I leave, someone repeats the ritualistic, "Make yourself at home here" to me.

I forgot. On our way there, we went down a street full of prostitutes. They stand behind blinds through which they can be seen, and for the most part they're charming looking. You discuss the price through openings in the blinds, which are painted all colors: greens, reds, yellows, sky blue. They are caged birds.

Then climbing up a little skyscraper. São Paulo in the night. The fairy tale aspect of modern cities with twinkling avenues and rooftops. Surrounded by coffee and orchids. But it's difficult to imagine.

Then Andrade tells me his theory: cannibalism as a vision of the world. Confronted with the failure of Descartes and science, return to the primitive fertilization: matriarchy and anthropophagy. Since the first bishop to arrive in Bahia was eaten, Andrade dates his review from the year 317, the year of the ingestion of Bishop Sardine (he was named Sardine).

Last hour. After my lecture, Andrade informs me that in the model penitentiary they have seen prisoners commit suicide by beating their heads against the walls and by closing drawers against their throats to the point of suffocation.

• AUGUST 5, AUGUST 6, AUGUST 7 (The trip to Iguape)[32]

We leave for the religious festivals of Iguape, but at 10 instead of 7 as planned. In fact we were supposed to drive all day inland, on the deplorable Brazilian roads, and it would have been better to arrive before nightfall. But there were delays, the car wasn't ready, etc. We leave São Paulo and begin driving south. The road, whether made of dirt or stone, is covered with red dust, and the vegetation on each side of the road for half a mile is covered with a layer of dried mud. After several miles we too—that is, the driver who looks like Auguste Comte; Andrade and his son, whose head is full of philosophers; Sylvestre, the French cultural attaché; and myself—are covered with the same dust. It gets in through every opening in the large Ford pickup truck and slowly fills up our noses and mouths. On top of it all a ferocious sun that roasts the earth and brings all life to a halt. After thirty miles, a disturbing noise. We stop. A spring in front is broken, visibly sticking out from the cluster of springs and brushing against the rim of the tire. Auguste Comte scratches his head and announces that we can get it fixed ten miles up the road. I advise him to take the broken spring out immediately before it gets wedged against the tire. But he's optimistic about it. We go another three miles and stop—the spring is stuck. Auguste Comte decides to get a tool: from a chest in the back of the truck, he pulls out a thick iron rod which he uses as a hammer, banging it harder and harder against the plate, imagining that he can force it loose.

I explain that there's a nut to take off and the tire itself. But finally I realize that he's set out on these bad roads for a long trip without a monkey wrench. We wait, beneath a sun that could kill, until finally a truck comes along, and the driver, thank goodness, has a monkey wrench. The tire is taken off, the nut unscrewed, and the plate of the spring is finally removed. We set out again between the pale, craggy mountains; from time to time we sight a starving water buffalo with an escort of sad vultures. At 1 o'clock we arrive in Piédade, an unpleasant little village, where we're warmly welcomed by the innkeeper Doña Anesia whom, at one time, Andrade must have courted. Served by Maria, an Indian métis, who ends up offering me artificial flowers. An interminable Brazilian meal which one manages to get down thanks to the *pinga*, which is the name of the local *cachasa*. In the meantime they've repaired the spring, and we leave. We're constantly ascending and the air is becoming very thin. There are immense uninhabited and uncultivated expanses. The terrible solitude of this unlimited wilderness explains certain things about this country. Arrive at Pilar at 3. But there Auguste Comte realizes that he's made a mistake. We're told that we've driven 40 miles too far. Which means, here, two or three hours of traveling. Our bodies aching from the bumpy ride, and covered with dust, we set off to find the right road. In fact, it's not until the end of the day that we begin to descend the other side of the Serra. I have time to see the first miles of virgin forest, the density of this sea of vegetation, to imagine the solitude in the middle of this unexplored world, and night falls as we plunge into the forest. We drive for hours, pitching and rocking along a narrow road that runs between walls of high trees, amid a thick, sugary odor. From time to time through the thickness of the forest, fireflies pass, and birds with red eyes brush against the windshield. Apart from that the immobility and muteness of this dreadful world are absolute, even though from time to time Andrade thinks he's heard an ocelot. The road weaves and winds, continues over bridges of swaying planks that cross little rivers. Then comes the fog and a fine rain that dissolves the light from our headlights. We're not driving, but literally creeping along. It's almost 7 P.M., we've been on the road since 10 A.M., and our fatigue is such that we receive with a certain fatalism Auguste Comte's announcement that we're running out of gas. However, the forest is not quite so thick—and slowly, the landscape is changing. We finally reach the open air and a small village where we're halted by a large river. Light signals on the other side and we see a large ferry boat approaching by means of rods pulled by mulattoes in straw hats, the oldest system there is.[33] We embark and the ferry drifts slowly across the Ribeira river. The river is wide and flows gently towards the sea and the night. On the banks the forest is still dense. Misty stars in the thick sky. On board nobody speaks. The absolute silence of the hour is broken only by the lapping of the river against the flanks of the ferry. In the bow of the ferry, I watch the river descend; the strangeness of this setting, which is nonetheless familiar. Bizarre bird cries and the call of bullfrogs rise from the two banks. At this exact moment it is midnight in Paris.

Disembarkment. Then we continue to creep towards Registro, a true Japanese capital in the middle of Brazil,[34] where I have the time to glimpse houses delicately decorated and even a kimono. We're told that Iguape is only 40 miles farther.

We set off again. A humid breeze, an incessant mist indicate that the sea is not far. The road becomes sand—more difficult and dangerous than it was before. It's midnight when we finally arrive at Iguape. Not counting stops, it took us ten hours to drive the 180 miles that separate us from São Paulo.

Everything is closed at the hotel. A distinguished townsman, whom we meet by chance in the night, takes us to the mayor's house (he's called the prefect here). Through the door the mayor tells us that we're sleeping at the hospital. Set off for the hospital. Despite my fatigue, the city seems to me to be beautiful, with its colonial churches, the nearby forest, its low, naked houses

and the thick softness of the damp air. Andrade
imagines that we can hear the sea. But it's far. At
the Happy Memory Hospital (that's its name), the
friendly city father leads us to a renovated ward
that smells of fresh paint from thirty yards away.[35]
We're told that in fact it's been repainted in our
honor. But there's no light: the local power plant
shuts down at 11 P.M. In the glow from our lighters
we nonetheless see six clean and simple beds. It's
our dormitory. We put down our suitcases. And
the city father wants us to join him for a sandwich
at his club. Exhausted, we go to the club.[36] The
club is a kind of second floor bistro where we meet
other distinguished persons who shower us with
their respects. Once again I notice the exquisite
Brazilian politeness, perhaps a bit ceremonious,
but still much better than the European tactless-
ness. Sandwich and beer. But a tall imbecile who
can hardly stand on his own feet is struck with the
curious idea of demanding to see my passport. I
show him my passport, and he tells me that it's invalid. Tired, I send him packing. Indignant, the
personages huddle together for a moment, and
then come over to tell me that they're going to put
this policeman (for that's what he is) in prison, and
that I will be able to choose the charges that I
want to press against him. I beg of them not to put
him in prison. They explain to me that this foul-
mouthed imbecile has disregarded the great honor

that I have done Iguape, and that his bad manners must be punished. I protest. But they're determined to honor me in this way. The affair lasts until the following evening when I finally find the right approach, asking them, as a personal favor to me, to spare this scatter-brained policeman. They proclaim my chivalry and tell me that it shall be done according to my wishes.[37]

In any case, the night of the drama we leave for the hospital and halfway there meet the mayor, who has gotten up to accompany us to our beds. He has also awakened the power plant personnel, and we have lights. They make sure we're comfortable almost to the point of tucking us in, and finally, at 1 A.M., overwhelmed with fatigue, we try to sleep. I say try because my bed slants a little and my neighbors turn from side to side and Auguste Comte snores ferociously. Finally, very late, I fall into a dreamless sleep.

• AUGUST 6

Wake up very early. Unfortunately, no water in this hospital. I shave and wash a little using mineral water. Then the personages arrive and take us to the main ward for breakfast. Finally, we go out into Iguape.

In the little garden of the Fountain,[38] soft and mysterious with clusters of flowers between the banana trees and the palms, I regain a little ease and tranquillity. In front of a grotto, some métis, mulattoes and the first gauchos that I've seen wait patiently to obtain some pieces of the "growing stone." In fact Iguape is a city where an effigy of the Good Jesus was found in the water by some fishermen who came to this grotto to wash it. Ever since, a stone grows there ineluctably, and people come to chisel off beneficent pieces of it. The city itself, between the forest and the river, is crowded around the large church of the Good Jesus. Several hundred houses in a single style—low, stuccoed, multicolored. Beneath the fine rain that soaks its badly paved streets, with the motley crowd—gauchos, Japanese, Indians, métis, elegant, distinguished persons—which is its population, Iguape bears the colonial stamp. The melancholy there is particular; it's the melancholy of places that are at the ends of the earth. Aside from the heroic route that we took, only two weekly flights connect Iguape to the rest of the world. One could find refuge here.

Throughout the day the kindness of our hosts is constant. But we've come for the procession. As soon as the afternoon begins firecrackers are going off everywhere, startling into flight the bald

vultures adorning the rooftops. The crowd gets
bigger. Some of these pilgrims have been travel-
ling the deplorable inland roads for five days. One
of them who looks Assyrian, with a beautiful black
beard, tells us that he was saved by the Good Jesus
from a shipwreck, after one night and one day
stranded in high seas, and that he has vowed to
carry a 130-pound stone on his head for the entire
procession.[39] The hour approaches. From the
church come penitents in surplices: first the
blacks, then the whites; then children dressed as
angels; then the "children of Mary"; then an effigy of the Good Jesus himself, behind which the
bearded man advances, barechested and carrying
an enormous slab on his head. Finally an orchestra
comes, playing a double-step and, at the end of the
procession, the crowd of pilgrims, which is the
only really interesting sight, the rest being ordi-
nary and rather sordid. But the crowd that pro-
ceeds down a narrow street, filling it almost to
bursting, is one of the strangest assemblages that
one could imagine. The ages, races, the colors of
the clothes, the classes, the infirmities, all are
mixed together in a gaudy, oscillating mass, lit up
at intervals by bursts of holy candles, above which
firecrackers explode incessantly. From time to
time an airplane—out of place in this ageless
world—also passes overhead. Mobilized for the
occasion, it rumbles by at regular intervals above

the personages in their elegance and the Good Jesus. We go to wait for the procession at another strategic point, and when it passes in front of us, the bearded man is wincing with fatigue and his legs are trembling. But he makes it to the end nonetheless. The bells ring, stores and houses on the route of the procession which had closed their doors and windows now open them—and we go to dinner.

After dinner, in the square the young gauchos sing, and everyone sits in a circle around them. The firecrackers continue, and a child gets a finger blown off. He cries and screams as they're taking him away. "Why did the Good Jesus do that?" (This cry of the soul is translated for me.)

I go right to bed because we're leaving early the next day. But the firecrackers and the horrendous sneezes of Auguste Comte keep me from falling asleep until very late.

• A U G U S T 7

Same road, but we avoid the detour of the other day, and we cross three rivers. Saw a hummingbird. And once again for hours I watch this monotonous nature and these immense spaces: one can't say they are beautiful, but they cling insistently to the soul. Country where the seasons are confused with one another, where the vegetation is so intertwined as to become formless, where bloods are so mixed up that the soul loses its borders. A loud splashing, the sea-green light of the forests, the varnish of red dust which covers all things, the melting of time, the slowness of the country, the brief and extravagant excitement of the big cities—it's the country of indifference and blood-explosions. Try as it might the skyscraper has yet to overcome the spirit of the forest — the immensity, the melancholy. Sambas—the authentic ones—best express what I mean.

But the last thirty miles are the most exhausting. Driving prudently, Auguste Comte lets everyone pass us. But each car raises so much red dust that the headlights can't penetrate this mineral fog and we have to stop the car. We no longer know where we are, and I feel my nostrils and mouth being pasted with suffocating mud. São Paulo, the hotel and a hot bath are a welcome relief.

• AUGUST 8

All the latitudes and longitudes which still lie before me make me nauseous. Gloomy, agitated day (I'm writing this in the plane that's flying me to

Fort Alesa). At 11 A.M. Brazilian philosophers come to ask me for several "explanations." Lunch at a young couple's house, both French professors. Charming. Then a visit to the Alliance Francaise. Walk with Mme. P. through the streets of São Paulo where I happen upon a photo of myself, which makes me feel modest. Cocktails at Valeur's. Dinner at Sylvestre's. Lecture. Once again the auditorium is packed and some people have to stand. A thoughtful French girl has brought me some *Gauloises*.[40] After the lecture I'm taken to a theater to hear a Brazilian woman sing. Then champagne at Andrade's. I return to the hotel drained and exhausted, tired of human faces.

• AUGUST 9

Andrade and Sylvestre are emotional, etc., as I depart for Porto Alegre. Lunch on the plane. For the first time a slight attack of asthma. But no one notices. In Porto Alegre it's bitter cold. Four or five frozen Frenchmen are waiting for me at the airport. They tell me that I'm supposed to lecture this evening, an event which was not scheduled. View from Kapotes[41]—the light is very beautiful. City ugly. Despite its five rivers. These islands of civilization are often hideous. Lecture in the evening. People are turned away. The press exaggerates it. But this amuses me more than anything else. I just want to leave and to finish with it, to finish once and for all. Someone notices that I don't have my visa for Chile. I have to stop at Montevideo, telegraph, etc.

• AUGUST 10

Walk in the city. At 2 P.M. the airplane, where I'm writing this and what precedes it. Terrible sadness and a feeling of isolation. My mail hasn't reached me and I'm traveling farther and farther away from it.

The French officials in Montevideo do not greet me warmly. My lecture dates had to be changed several times. But I wasn't responsible for that. They've even neglected to reserve a room for me. I wind up, feeling blue, in a kind of closet —where nonetheless I feel better by myself than I did before with those who were forced to be my hosts. I stay up late, pacing the room, and concentrating my will on not weakening psychically before the end of the trip.

Obliged to admit that for the first time in my life I feel myself in the middle of a psychological collapse. Despite all my efforts this delicate balance, which up until now has withstood everything, is being upset. There are glaucous waters within me where vague forms pass, diluting my energies. In a way this depression is hellish. If my hosts here knew the effort I was making just to seem normal, they would at least make an effort to smile from time to time.

• AUGUST 11

Wake up early, write some letters. Then, with no news from my official chaperones, I go out into a beautiful, icy day to look around Montevideo. The tip of the city is bathed by the yellow waters of the La Plata river. Airy and orderly, Montevideo is surrounded by a necklace of beaches and a maritime boulevard which I find rather beautiful. There's comfort in this city, which seems easier to live in than others I've seen. Mimosas in the residential neighborhoods; palms make me think of Menton. Also relieved to be in a Spanish-speaking country. Return to the hotel. My official chaperones wake up. I'll leave this evening for Buenos Aires on the La Plata riverboat. Lunch at the cultural attaché's house. Quai d'Orsay and flowery stupidities. In the evening the boat leaves Montevideo. Once again I watch the moon on the muddy waters. But my heart is colder than it was on the *Campana*.

• AUGUST 12

Morning. Buenos Aires. Enormous accumulation of houses jutting out. W.R. is waiting for me. We discuss the question of lectures. I hold firm, adding that my lecture, if I give it, will be in part about freedom of expression. He supposes that, like everything else, my lecture could be subjected to a preliminary reading by the censors, and I warn him that I would flatly refuse. In that case he's of the opinion that it's better not to go looking for trouble.[42] Same for the ambassador. Tour of the city—exceptionally ugly. Some people in the afternoon. I end up at V.O.'s.[43] Large, pleasant house in the *Gone with the Wind* style. Grand and old luxury. I want to lie down there and sleep until the end of the world. In fact, I do fall asleep.

• AUGUST 13

Good night. I awake to a cold, hazy day. From her bedroom V. sends me some letters. Then the newspapers. The Peronist press either ignored or softened the declaration I made yesterday afternoon. Lunch with the director of the *Prensa* (opposition newspaper), police proceedings, etc. Afternoon, forty people. Leaving there, dinner with V. and talk until midnight. She plays Britten's *Rape of Lucretia* and some recordings of Baudelaire's poems—wonderful. First evening of real relaxation since my departure. I should stay here until the day I return—to avoid the continual struggle that is exhausting me. There is a temporary peace in this house.

• AUGUST 14

At 9 A.M. no news about the airplane that's supposed to take me to Chile. At noon they call. Day spent at V.'s waiting to leave. Rafael Alberti is there, with his wife. Nice. I know that he's a Communist. Finally I explain my point of view to him. And he agrees with me. But one day slander will separate me from this man who should remain a comrade. What's to be done? We're in the age of separation. Finally, at sunset, the airplane leaves. We pass the Andes at night (the symbol of this trip), and I see nothing. At most, I catch sight of the snow-covered ridges in the dark. But I had time before nightfall to see the immense and monotonous pampas—endless. Through a velvety sky the descent into Santiago is done in a flash. At our feet a forest of blinking stars. Caressing softness of these cities, which are spread out in the night along the edge of oceans.

• AUGUST 15

On the Pacific with Charvet and Fron. Ch. talks to
me about the influence of earthquakes on the Chi-
leans' behavior. Five hundred quakes per year—of
which several are catastrophic. This creates a psychology of instability. The Chilean is a gambler,
spends everything he makes, and indulges in capri-
cious politics.

We drive: the Pacific covered with long white
rolls. Santiago tucked in between the waters and
the Andes—violent colors (the marigolds are rust-
colored), flowering plum and almond trees stand
out against a background of snowy peaks—wonderful country.

Afternoon: bushed. At six, a symposium
where I'm in good shape. Dinner at Charvet's
where I'm completely depressed. From fatigue I
drink too much and go to bed late. Wasted time.

• AUGUST 16

Infernal day. Radio, tourism. Lunch with Vincent
Anidobre's son in a little house at the foot of the
Andes. Symposium here with some theater people.
At 7 P.M. a lecture which is tiring because the audi-
torium is so dense with people. Dinner at the em-

bassy. I was bored to tears. Only the ambassador is amusing; yesterday he took off his jacket and danced.

• AUGUST 17

Day of disturbances and riots. Yesterday there were demonstrations. But today, it's like an earthquake overtaking them. The issue is a price increase for the "micros" (Santiago's buses). They turn the buses over and set them on fire. They break the windows of passing ones. In the afternoon I'm told that the university, where the students were demonstrating, has been closed—and that my lecture won't take place. Within two hours the French department has organized a lecture at the French Institute. When I leave there, stores have barred their windows and armed, helmeted troops literally occupy the city. Sometimes shooting into the air. It's a state of siege. During the night I hear isolated shots.

• AUGUST 18

Airplane is late, won't take off until nighttime. The Andes are blocked. I sleep badly or very little here—and I'm tired. The Charvets come for me at eleven, and I'm asleep on my feet. But their kindness is not burdensome, and we drive through the Chilean countryside. The mimosas and the weeping willows. Beautiful, strong nature. We stop for an excellent lunch, eaten in front of a fireplace. Then we fork off towards the Andes, and we stop for a snack at a mountain hotel, once again in front of a beautiful fire. I feel good in Chile and under different circumstances could live here a little while. When we return, we learn that the airplane has been postponed until tomorrow. It's pouring. Dinner at the Charvets'. Go to bed at midnight. At the hotel I find goodbye presents. It takes me a long time to fall asleep.

• AUGUST 19

At 4:30 A.M. the airline company telephones me. I should be at the field at 6. At 7 the airplane takes off. But, after looking for a way through, it descends toward the south and at the end of a 125-mile detour enters another pass. The Andes: prodigious, shattered reliefs, tearing through mountains of clouds—but the snow dazzles me. We pitch and roll incessantly and in addition, I suffer a fit of asthma. I narrowly avoid the worst —and pretend to be sleeping.

It's noon by the time we reach Buenos Aires. At this moment the lack of sleep is overwhelming.

V.O. has come to pick me up, but there's no one from the embassy, and they haven't reserved me a ticket for Montevideo, where I'm supposed to speak at 6:30. Thanks to V. we get to Buenos Aires quickly and then to the seaplane terminal. There are no seats available. V. telephones a friend. Everything is arranged. I leave at 4:45 in overcast, yellow weather above yellow waters. At 6:15, Montevideo. The embassy has sent someone who tells me that they have decided to cancel the lecture and to take me to the French high school instead. There the director tells me that some people have shown up anyway, and that he doesn't know what to do. I suggest a debate, even though I'm exhausted. They accept and schedule two lectures for me for the next day, one at 11, the other at 6. Debate. And I go to bed, drunk with fatigue.

• AUGUST 20

Brutal day. 10 A.M. journalists and A.; at 11, the first lecture, in an auditorium at the University. In the middle of the lecture a strange character enters the auditorium. A cape, short beard, a dark gaze. He stands at the back of the room, and conspicuously opens a magazine and reads it. From time to time he coughs loudly. He, at least, adds some life to the auditorium. A moment with José Bergamín,[44] refined, face deeply etched, with the worn-out look of a Spanish intellectual. He doesn't want to choose between Catholicism and Communism as long as the Spanish war is not over. A hypertense man whose energy is purely spiritual. I love this kind of man.

Bergamín: my most profound temptation is suicide. And spectacular suicide. (Return to Spain at the risk of being condemned, resist, and die.)

Lunch with several nice couples, professors of French. At 4, press conference. At 5, I see the director of the theater that's going to put on *Caligula*. He wants to stick some ballet in it. It's an international mania. At 6, Miss Lussitch and the charming lady who is the cultural attaché from Uruguay take me for a short drive through the gardens at the entrance to the city. The evening is soft, short, slightly tender. This country is simple and beautiful. I relax a little. At 6:30, second lecture. The ambassador felt obliged to come with his better half. Seated in the first row are the sinister faces of boredom and vulgarity. After the lecture, I take a walk with Bergamín. We end up in a crowded cafe. He doubts the effectiveness of what he's doing. I tell him that uncompromisingly sustaining a refusal is a positive act whose consequences are also positive.—Then dinner at Suzannah Soca's. A crowd of worldly women who become unmanageable after the third whiskey. Several of them literally proposition me. But they aren't even tempting. A French lady manages to construct an apology for Franco in front of me. Exhausted, I lay into her—and realize that I'd better leave. I ask the cultural attaché to have a drink with me, and we escape. At least this pretty face helps me with the struggle of living. The light lies softly on Montevideo. A pure sky, the rustling of dry palms above Constitution Place, pigeons taking flight, white in the black sky. The hour would be simple and my solitude—18 days without news, without intimacy—could be eased a little. But my charming companion starts reciting for me, in the middle of the square, some French verses she has written, miming the tragic style, arms crossed on her breast, voice rising and falling. I wait it out. Then we go have a drink and I take her home. I go to bed, but anxiety and melancholy keep me from sleeping.

• AUGUST 21

Out of bed at 8 A.M. I slept 3 or 4 hours. But the airplane is taking off at 11. Beneath a tender, fresh, cloudy sky, Montevideo unrolls its beaches —charming city where everything implies happiness—and a spiritless happiness. Stupidity of these airplane trips—barbarian and regressive means of transportation. At 5 P.M. we fly over Rio and, getting off the plane, I am welcomed by this close, humid air—the consistency of cotton-wool—which I had forgotten and which is peculiar to Rio. At the same time, shrill and multicolored parrots and a peacock with a discordant voice. Barely capable of going to bed, and still without news, since there was no mail waiting for me at the embassy.

• AUGUST 22

They bring me my mail; it had been sitting for 18 days in some office. Tired, I stay in my room all day. Evening, a lecture, after which a drink at Mme. Mineur's. Go to bed with a fever.

• AUGUST 23

Get up a little better. My departure is approaching. It'll be Thursday or Saturday. I think of Paris as if it were a monastery. Lunch at Copacabana facing the sea. The waves are high and supple. It relaxes me a little to watch them. Return to the hotel. I sleep a little. At 5, public debate with the Brazilian students. Is it the fatigue? It's never been so easy for me. Dinner at the Claveries' with Mme. R., ravishing woman but, it seems to me, without depth.

• A U G U S T 2 4

I get up feeling even better than yesterday. The departure has now been set for Saturday. Visitors in the morning and the fatigue returns. To the extent that I decide not to have lunch. At 1:30 Pedrosa and his wife come to take me to see paintings by the insane, in a suburban hospital of modern lines and ancient filth. My heart contracts seeing faces behind the tall, barred windows. Two interesting painters. Without a doubt the others have what it takes to send progressive Parisian minds into ecstasy. But, in fact, it's ugliness. Even more striking in the ugly and vulgar sculptures. I'm appalled when I recognize a psychiatrist from the hospital as the young man who, in the beginning, asked me the most idiotic question I was asked in all of South America. He's the one who decides the fate of these unfortunate people. Moreover, he's in the advanced stages of illness himself. But I'm even more appalled when he tells me that he's going to make the trip to Paris with me on Saturday. Enclosed with him in a metal cabin for 36 hours—this is the final ordeal.

In the evening, dinner at Pedrosa's with some intelligent people. Driving rain as I return to the hotel.

• AUGUST 25

Grippe. Without a doubt I'm not suited to this climate. I work a little during the morning, then go to the zoo to see the sloth.

But the sloth is at liberty and one is obliged to look for him in the park's thousands of trees. I let it drop. Splendid ocelots at least; hideous lizards and the anteater. Lunch with Letarget at Copacabana. Rio is veiled by an incessant rain that fills the holes in the roads and sidewalks and dissolves the false gloss with which they have tried to cover it. The colonial city reappears and I must say it's more attractive like this with its mud, its trampling, its steamy sky. Errands in the afternoon. Everything I find in this country comes from somewhere else. At 5 o'clock in the evening, at the Mendès' house. Once again a huge crowd and I'm bored without having the strength to hide it. Physically, I can no longer endure large gatherings of people. Same thing at dinner where there are seven of us—when I thought it would only be Pedrosa and Barleto—where everyone, by increasing the amplitude of his voice, interrupts everyone else. With my grippe on top of it all, the ordeal becomes infernal. I would like to go back to the hotel, but I don't dare say so. At 1 A.M., Mme. Pedrosa sees that I can't keep my eyes open, and I go to bed.

• AUGUST 26 AND 27

Two frightful days where I drag about with my
grippe to different places and people, blind to
what I see, preoccupied with regaining my
strength, amidst people who, from friendship or
hysteria, perceive nothing of the state I'm in and
thus make it a little worse. Evening at the consul's
where I hear someone comment that corporal
punishment is a necessity in our colonial armies.

Saturday 4 P.M. I'm notified that the airplane
motor has broken down and that the departure
has been moved to tomorrow, Sunday. The fever
increases and I begin to wonder if it's not a question of something more than the grippe.

• AUGUST 31

Sick. Bronchitis at least. They telephone that
we're leaving this afternoon. The day is radiant.
Doctor. Penicillin. The trip ends in a metallic cof-
fin between an insane doctor and a diplomat,
heading towards Paris.

Notes—United States

1. Camus makes the trip as a journalist.
2. Port in Saudi Arabia where foreign diplomatic corps are stationed.
3. It later becomes known that the positions taken by *Combat*, the Resistance newspaper that Camus edited, are the source of this suspicion.
4. An Italian critic and writer, a friend of Albert Camus.
5. O'Brien translated the works of Camus in the U.S.A.
6. American publisher.
7. Knopf was to become Camus's principal publisher.
8. Lionel Abel, writer and journalist, who translated Camus's lecture at Harvard.

9. Waldo Franck, American writer who had a long correspondence with Camus.
10. American painter (1847–1917). Exhibited at the Metropolitan Museum in New York.
11. Painter from Uruguay. Friend of Bonnard.
12. This is already the theme of *The Rebel*.
13. One finds this disagreement with modern existentialism in the letter to the director of the Nef. (*Pléiade*, I, p. 1745, January 1946).
14. One finds echoes of this preoccupation in *State of Siege*.
15. Young American who offered Camus, with great discretion, free use of his apartment whenever he wanted it.
16. Cf. "La Mer au plus près" (*Pléiade*, II, p. 879): "On certain days in New York, lost at the bottom of those stone and steel shafts where millions of men wander, I would run from one shaft to the next, without seeing where they ended, until, exhausted, I was sustained only by the human mass seeking its way out." (Translated as "The Sea Close By" in *Lyrical and Critical Essays*, New York: Knopf, 1969, p. 173.)
17. "The Rains of New York" (Forms and Colors, 1947), (*Pléiade*, II, p. 1829).
18. Camus will give this trait to Tarrou's father (*Pléiade*, I, p. 1420).
19. A recurrent theme in *Neither Victims nor Executioners (Ni Victimes ni Bourreaux, Pléiade*, II, p. 332ff.).

Notes—South America

1. Name that Camus gave his car.
2. Cf. "La Mer au plus près" (*Pléiade*, II, p. 880): "From time to time the waves lap against the bow; a bitter, unctuous foam, the gods' saliva, flows along the wood and loses itself in the water, where it scatters into shapes that die and are reborn, the hide of some white and blue cow, an exhausted beast that floats for a long time in our wake." (Translated as "The Sea Close By" in *Lyrical and Critical Essays*, New York: Knopf, 1969, p. 174.)
3. Cf. "La Mer au plus près," p. 882: "At last, at its zenith, it lights a whole corridor of sea, a rich river of milk which, with the motion of the ship, streams down inexhaustibly toward us across the dark ocean." (Knopf, p. 176.)

4. Cf. "La Mer au plus près," p. 880: "Thus, throughout the morning, we hear our sails slapping above a cheerful pond. The waters are heavy, scaly, covered with cool froth." (Knopf, p. 174.)
5. Cf. "La Mer au plus près," p. 881: "After an hour's cooking, the pale water, a vast white-hot iron sheet, sizzles. In a minute it will turn and offer its damp side, now hidden in waves and darkness, to the sun." (Knopf, p. 175.)
6. Camus is referring to an area in the southern Atlantic renowned for its lack of wind. The term derives from navigators' slang, signifying a place from which one can not move. Aviators use the term to refer to poor visibility due to fog.
7. A region of mountains in Algeria.
8. French author (1888–1948).
9. Daniel Halévy, French historian (1872–1962).
10. Without a doubt this is a memory from his trip to Mallorca in the summer of 1935, mixed with the memory of nationalist repression in Mallorca which is denounced by Bernanos in *A Diary of My Times.*
11. Belgian poet (1899–1984). Author of *A Barbarian in Asia* (1933).
12. Uruguayan-born French poet, dramatist, and novelist (1884–1960). His works include *The Colonel's Children* (poetry, 1926), *Bolivar* (play, 1936), and *Along the Road to Bethlehem* (novel, 1933).
13. Swiss critic, translator, and editor (1901–1957). Béguin translated Hoffmann and Goethe into French.
14. Was the lover of Auguste Comte, whom she met in 1844.

15. Cf. "The Growing Stone" in *Exile and the Kingdom*. The macumba scene is taken from three journal fragments.
16. Cf. "La Pierre qui Pousse" ("The Growing Stone"), *Pléiade*, I, p. 1674.
17. *Ibid*, p. 1664.
18. *Ibid*, p. 1675.
19. *Ibid*, p. 1675. Most of the paragraph is used.
20. *Ibid*, p. 1676. This time it is about a black woman.
21. French historian (1878–1956).
22. One sees here the reappearance of the obsession with the Cold War which creates two opposing camps, and the idea of an intermediary force which would balance them.
23. Bay of the state of Bahia.
24. Approximate quotation from *Actuelles I*.
25. B.: probably Belcourt, a suburb of Algiers.
26. Camus had written: "in fact, this is how I speak, *with more clarity and violence than ever before.*"
27. This *candomblé* appears in "The Growing Stone," where it is grafted onto the macumba.
28. French poet (1907–   ). Author of *Hypnos Waking: Poetry and Prose* (1956).
29. Camus had published an introduction to Chamfort in 1944 (cf. *Pléiade*, II, p. 1099).
30. The Minas Gerais, a state in central Brazil.
31. There is an allusion to this visit in the *Diario de São Paulo* from August 6, 1949.
32. The story "The Growing Stone" is set in Iguape.
33. Cf. "La Pierre qui Pousse," p. 1675.
34. Cf. "La Pierre qui Pousse," p. 1659.
35. *Ibid*, p. 1660.
36. *Ibid*, p. 1662.

37. All of this episode is taken up again in "La Pierre qui Pousse," pp. 1664 and 1672.
38. Cf. "La Pierre qui Pousse," p. 1667.
39. This is the character called "the cook." The rest of the text is found in a transposed form, p. 1680 ff.
40. Cheap, trendy French cigarettes.
41. Camus may have meant Kapok.
42. Cf. above, pp. 96–97.
43. Victoria Ocampo.
44. Spanish philosopher and essayist.

Chronology

11.7.13. Birth of Albert Camus at Mondovi, Constantine, French North Africa.

10.11.14. Lucien Camus, his father, is killed at the first Battle of the Marne. His mother, née Catherine Sintès, goes to live in Belcourt, a working-class suburb of Algiers. She works as a charwoman to provide for Camus and his elder brother Lucien, who are brought up largely by their maternal grandmother.

1918–1923. Camus attends the *école communale* of Belcourt. His Nobel Prize speech of 1957 is dedicated to his teacher, Louis Germain.

1923. Wins scholarship to the lycée in Algiers (now Lycée Albert Camus).

1928–1930. Is goalkeeper for the Racing Universitaire d'Alger.

1930. First attack of tuberculosis.

1933. First marriage, to Simone Hie.

1934. Joins Communist Party. Works on the Arab question. Laval's visit to Moscow in 1935 brings about a change in the Party line, and Camus begins to feel critical. He did not, however, according to Roger Quilliot, actually leave the Party until 1937, the date at which the Théâtre du Travail, which he had been instrumental in founding, broke its Communist links and became the Théâtre de L'Equipe.

1935. Begins the *cahiers*. Completes his *licence de philosophie* (B.A.) in June. Plays an active part in the Communist *Maison de la Culture* in Algiers. Cooperates in writing *Révolte dans les Asturies,* a play about the revolt of the Oviedo miners in Spain. The play was not allowed to be publicly performed but was privately published. Begins research on Plotinus, for his *diplôme d'études supérieures* (roughly an M.A. by thesis). During the whole of this time he is supporting himself by various jobs, and works for the Institut de Météorologie.

1936. May. Successfully presents his thesis, on Néo-Platonisme et Pensée Chrétienne. Begins to work as an actor for the touring company of Radio Algiers. His first marriage is dissolved. In the summer, travels to Austria and returns via Prague and Italy.

1937. Publication of *L'Envers et L'Endroit* (written 1935–6). Compelled to go to Embrun, in France, for reasons of health in summer, and again travels back through Italy. Refuses a post as teacher in Sidi-bel-Abbès. Breaks with Communist Party.

1938. Foundation, in October, of *Alger-Républicain,* an independent left-wing paper edited by Pascal Pia. Camus joins the staff, and his first article appears on October 10, 1938. He reviews books regularly, but also writes a large number of other articles. Completes first version of *Caligula*.

1939. January–March. Series of articles in *Alger-Républicain* leading to the acquittal of Michel Hodent. July. Publication of eleven articles on Kabylia, describing the poverty of the area and criticizing government policy. The more important of these were republished in *Actuelles III* in 1938, and some were translated in *Resistance, Rebellion, and Death* in 1960.

1939. September. Camus made editor of the evening paper *Le Soir-Républicain,* where he signs a number of articles Jean Mersault. Publication of *Noces.* Rejected for military service for reasons of health.

1940. January–February. Both *Soir-Républicain* and *Alger-Républicain* cease to appear. Camus is unable to find a job in Algeria because of his political affiliations, and goes to Paris, where Pascal Pia finds him a place in *Paris-Soir.* Camus contributed no articles to this paper, which he disliked, and worked only as a typesetter.

1940. June. Leaves Paris with *Paris-Soir* and goes to Clermont-Ferrand. Then to Bordeaux and Lyons. December. Second marriage, to Francine Faure.

1941. Return to Oran. Teaches for a short time in a private school. Completes *Le Mythe de Sisyphe.*
December 19. Execution of Gabriel Péri—an event which, according to Camus himself, crystallized his revolt against the Germans.

1942. Return to France. July. Publication of *L'Etranger.* Camus joins the resistance network *Combat* in the Lyons region. January. New attack of tuberculosis.

1943. Publication of *Le Mythe de Sisyphe.* First of the *Lettres à un Ami Allemand* (translated in *Resistance, Rebellion, and Death*). *Combat* sends him to Paris, where he is by now well known in literary circles. He becomes a publisher's reader and permanent member of the administrative staff at Gallimard. In order to avoid ever feeling that he had to publish books in order to earn his living, Camus kept this job until the end of his life.

1944. August. Editor of *Combat*. His unsigned, and supposedly anonymous, editorials are characteristic of the hopes and aspirations of the liberation period, and, coming after the first performance, in June 1944, of *Le Malentendu* (written 1942–1943), emphasized the dual nature of his attitude toward the world.

1945. Still with *Combat*, though writing less frequently. First performance of *Caligula*, in September, with Gérard Philipe in title role. Publication of *Lettres à un Ami Allemand* and of *La Remarque sur la Révolte*, starting point of *L'Homme Révolté*. Birth of his twin children, Catherine and Jean.

1946. Visit to America. (Camus tours New England, New York and Washington, D.C.) Completion of *La Peste*.

1947. June. Publication of *La Peste*. Great success. On June 3, 1947, Camus leaves *Combat*, whose financial difficulties no longer allow an independent editorial policy.

1948. October. First performance of *L'État de Siège*.

1949. June–August. Lecture tour in South America, described in detail in *American Journals*. Camus falls ill, and has to spend a long time convalescing.

1950. Publication of *Actuelles I*. Performance of *Les Justes*.

1951. *L'Homme Révolté*.

1952. Public quarrel with Sartre.

1953. Replaces Marcel Herrand as producer at the Festival d'Angers. *Actuelles II*.

1954. Publication of *L'Eté*, a collection of essays written between 1939 and 1954. Includes *Le Minotaure ou la Halte d'Oran*, many passages of which were first written in the *Carnets*. (Cf. English translation by Justin O'Brien in the volume containing the 1955 English translation of *Le Mythe de Sisyphe*.)

1955. Travels to Greece. Goes back to journalism in *L'Express* to support the election campaign of Mendès-France. Appeals for an agreement by both sides in the Algerian War to respect the civilian population.

1956. Publication of *La Chute*. Adaptation of Faulkner's *Requiem for a Nun*.

1957. Publication of the short stories *L'Exil et le Royaume*. Publication of the *Réflexions sur la Guillotine*, in a companion volume with Arthur Koestler's *Reflections on Hanging*. Awarded the Nobel Prize for Literature.

1958. Publication of *Actuelles III*. Articles on Algeria dating from 1939–58.

1959. Adaptation of Dostoevsky's *The Possessed*. Camus continues work on his projected novel *Le Premier Homme*.

1960. January 5. Killed in an automobile accident.

The two most useful studies on Camus's life are by Roger Quilliot, *La Mer et les Prisons* (Gallimard, 1956), and by Germaine Brée, *Camus* (Rutgers, 1959).

A Note on the Author

Albert Camus was born on November 7, 1913 in Mondovi, Algeria. His father, an itinerant agricultural worker, was killed on the Marne in 1914; his Spanish mother worked as a charwoman. While a student at Algiers University, Camus became active in the propaganda war against international fascism and protested the French establishment's treatment of the Arab population. Before the outbreak of World War II, Camus had already established a reputation as co-founder (director, actor, writer, theorist) of a theater for the proletariat, and as an essayist. Unable to find a job in Algeria due to his political affiliations, he moved to France in 1942, where he assumed editorship of the Resistance newspaper *Combat* until 1947.

Throughout his career, his writings addressed contemporary political and moral issues (fascism, genocide, colonialism, and political repression), as well as philosophical questions, such as the absurdity of modern life. He is considered by many to be the subtlest and most profound seeker of a valid liberal humanism in the twentieth century.

Camus's major works include *The Myth of Sisyphus* and *The Rebel* (essays); *Caligula* and *State of Siege* (drama); and *The Stranger* and *The Plague* (novels). He won the Nobel Prize for Literature in 1957. He died on January 5, 1960, in an automobile accident.

A Note on the Type

The text of *American Journals* was set in Baskerville, a slight modification of the classic face designed by the Englishman John Baskerville in the middle of the 18th century. It was during this period that a new handwriting style, the roundhand, was developed by scribes using the traditional broad-nibbed pens but changing the writing angle, keeping the flat edge of the pen parallel to the baseline. This made the down-stroke main line the heaviest and the horizontal lines the lightest. Baskerville's transitional roman design is more regimented than the old style, maintaining the consistency of each line stroke and ending with fine, tapered serifs. The Baskerville type style has greater contrast between capital and lowercase letters than most other roman faces, resulting in a higher degree of readability. The text was typeset by Computer Composition Corporation (Madison Heights, Michigan).